The *Abalone King* OF

MONTEREY

"POP" ERNEST DOELTER, PIONEERING JAPANESE FISHERMEN
& THE CULINARY CLASSIC THAT SAVED AN INDUSTRY

TIM THOMAS

AMERICAN PALATE

Published by American Palate
A Division of The History Press
Charleston, SC 29403
www.historypress.net

Cover images: Front: Abalone divers (top). *Kodani Family Collection*; abalone in seaweed (bottom). *John Cox*. Back: *Pat Sands Collection* (top); *Jerry Loomis* (bottom).

First published 2014

Manufactured in the United States

ISBN 978.1.60949.469.8

Library of Congress CIP data applied for.

Contents

Foreword

Yes, It Happened
in Monterey

Abalone! Abalone is a favorite food for several marine animals, including the sea otter. These tool-using mammals use rocks to crack the shell of the delicious, succulent abalone. But the real story is of how people have used, discovered and rediscovered the abalone and invented new methods of preparation to consume this much sought-after gastropod mollusk. And that story centers on the pioneering restaurateur of California who single-handedly made abalone the quintessential prize of California coastal cuisine and of diners throughout the nation. This delicacy soon became the subject of song and celebration and was the basis of a major seafood and tourist industry.

Historian Tim Thomas's account of the exceptional entrepreneur "Pop" Ernest, his life and his transformation of the richly flavored abalone to the American dining palate is one of the most amazing histories not only of restaurants and dining but also of California's scenic Central Coast. The story centers on the uniquely situated and picturesque seaside town of Monterey, as well as on the inventive ventures of Pop, this most enterprising European immigrant who took the abalone, already important in the diet of native Indian peoples of the California coast and of Japanese and other immigrant groups, and created a culinary sensation in Monterey and beyond.

In this book, Pop's amazing life and work as the "Abalone King" is lovingly told by Thomas. With many little-known or newly discovered accounts of Pop's life and how he launched the abalone into glory, Thomas recounts—after in-depth research and with great storytelling ability—the Pop Ernest story.

FOREWORD

Enjoy this book and look fondly when you gaze at the beautiful abalone steak on your plate the next time you venture to your local restaurant. Remember who made it possible: the Abalone King.

DENNIS COPELAND
Historian
City of Monterey

Preface

Sometime in the summer or fall of 1908, Chef "Pop" Ernest Doelter introduced his newest recipe, the abalone steak, in his small, picturesque Monterey restaurant. Unfortunately, we don't know who the first person was, or even what he or she felt, when that first bite was taken. What we do know is that soon after that first bite, the Café Ernest on Alvarado Street became known up and down the California coast, and people came from all over to eat his delicious new food sensation, "abalone." The demand was so big, and the restaurant so crowded, that all five of Chef Doelter's children were put to work serving abalone to patrons.

Ernst Ludwig Doelter first came to United States in March 1881, arriving at New York City. Doelter marked his birthdate as July 4, 1864, making him just seventeen years old. Born to a building contractor in Kehl, Germany, the opportunities for a young man looking to make his mark in the world must have been slim, as he and his older sister, Ida, set sail for the United States, leaving their two younger brothers, Albert and Otto, in Germany.

Life for a young German immigrant in New York City in the 1880s was hard. But Ernst found work in the many restaurants of New York City, learning the trade from the ground up. It's not known which restaurants he worked in, but for the next five years, he was a busboy, a dishwasher and a waiter, eventually making his way to the kitchens to learn the chef's trade. Although abalone is found all over the world, it is not found on the East Coast, so it is doubtful that that he had any experience with the shellfish that would eventually make him famous.

PREFACE

When he received his naturalization papers on January 26, 1887, Doelter identified his occupation as a baker. He also dropped Ludwig from his name and added an *e* to Ernst to Americanize his name, becoming Ernest Doelter.

So, just what is an abalone? An abalone is a big marine snail or gastropod from the genus *Haliotis*. Abalone may be found in most oceans of the world, usually in cold waters, off the Southern Hemisphere coasts of New Zealand, South Africa and Australia, as well as the Pacific coasts of western North America and Japan in the Northern Hemisphere.

Abalone goes by many names—sea ears, ear shells, Venus's ears and muttonfish. In Mexico, it's called *orejas de mar*, and in Japan, it's known as *awabi*. But the name *abalone* comes from Monterey, and it originated with the Rumsiens, the native people of Monterey, who had a word for the red abalone, the largest of the abalone and the predominate abalone in the Monterey Bay. That word is *aulun*. Early Spanish settlers called it *abulon*, based on the Rumsien word, and linguists today trace the word *abalone* all the way back to that word, *aulun*, that started in Monterey several thousand years ago.

The story of Pop Ernest Doelter, the "Abalone King," and the Monterey Japanese abalone industry is a unique and sometimes complicated story and one that would have been impossible to tell without a number of folks who helped me along the way. First and foremost is Patricia Sands, daughter of Carl and Pop's granddaughter, who graciously opened the family archives to me. Fred Brown, grandson to Pop, shared his mother Mimi's George Sterling poem. The late Roy Hattori spent hours and hours with me answering all my questions. I'd also like to thank Dennis Copeland, historian and archivist with the City of Monterey, and Ann Vileisis, who is writing her own book on abalone and shared some of her research with me. I thank Art Seavey, Joe Cavanaugh and Trevor Fay of the Monterey Abalone Company; David and Earl Ebert of US Abalone; Mary Alice Fettis, daughter of Sal Cerrito; Chef John Pisto; Jerry Loomis; historian Sandy Lydon for all the amazing work he has done on the Monterey Japanese story; Point Lobos curator Kurt Loesch; and historians Geoffrey Dunn, Kent Seavey, Erica J. Peters, Margo McBane and Micki Downey, who shared some of her work on the Masons. I'd also like to thank my friends in Japan: Yoshie Mitsuhashi, Toshio Oba and Toshio Takanashi. And last but not least, I want to thank Linda Yamane, who understood the importance of this story and encouraged me to finish it. This book is dedicated to the entire Doelter family.

Because of space limitations, I wasn't able to include all my references but you can contact me at timsardine@yahoo.com, and I will send them to you.

Chapter 1

A Little Abalone History

A balone has been gathered for thousands of years in the Monterey Bay area. The Rumsien people were the first to capitalize on this bounty. Abalone played a very important part in their lives. They ate it; used the shells to make tools like fishhooks, shovels and bowls; made beautiful abalone pendants to decorate baskets; made jewelry; and traded it to other California Indians for things they couldn't get in Monterey, like obsidian, a volcanic rock that they were using to make spear and arrow points. Abalone was traded (and has been found) from California all the way to the midwestern states.

The Rumsien were also the first abalone divers in the Monterey Bay. We know that from burials found around the Monterey Peninsula in recent years. The males have what's known as exostosis, or "surfers ear," a little bony growth that will cover the opening of the ear, eventually constricting the ear canal. This happens when you spend a lot of time in cold waters like the Monterey Bay. Burials have been discovered where the decedent was found wearing what can only be described as an "abalone skirt"—a dress made of abalone. The middens (also known as kitchen midden) are refuse dumps around the Monterey Peninsula that are so rich with abalone particles that they're called "abalone pavement."

When Monterey was part of Spanish empire, from 1770 to 1822, Russian otter hunters almost completely wiped out the abalone in the bay. They gathered as much abalone as they could, storing them in ship holds and piling them on the decks of their ships, and sailed to the Pacific Northwest to trade to the Indians for sea otter pelts.

When Mexico declared its independence from Spain in 1822, and Monterey became part of Mexico (1822–46), it opened the ports and allowed ships and trade from all over the world. Otter hunters and sealers arrived who took so many sea otters that they were virtually hunted to extinction. For the abalone, that was a good thing. Sea otters are the natural enemy to the abalone. Because there were very few otters, the abalone thrived in the bay. There are some accounts of people living in Monterey at that time collecting abalone, placing them in sacks, pounding them on the rocks until they were essentially jelly and then eating them.

In the early 1850s, a small group of Chinese fishermen and their families arrived in the Monterey Bay area having sailed across the Pacific in three small thirty- to fifty-foot junks. There's a series of currents that pushed them across the Pacific—the Chinese called it the "black tide" or the "big drain." It comes out near Cape Mendocino in Northern California, turns southward and runs down the California coast; eventually, they landed near Point Lobos, about ten miles south of Monterey. These Chinese voyagers were taken in by a nearby Rumsien village and nursed back to health. Afterward, the newcomers looked out into the Monterey Bay, where they saw that no one was fishing out there. They also saw the abundance of abalone.

Abalone is a special food item to the Chinese. In China at that time, it was illegal for Chinese peasants to gather it. Since no such laws existed in Monterey, a thriving industry was born. Soon word spread to the Chinese communities all over California, resulting in Chinese flocking to the area. One newspaper referred to it as the "Abalone Rush." By 1879, more than 4 million pounds of abalone had been harvested by Chinese fishermen. The Chinese fishing methods for abalone included collecting them from the intertidal areas at low tide or by boat, using a viewing box (a pyramid-shaped box usually made of redwood with a piece of glass at the wide end that the fisherman could look through to spot the abalone). They also employed a long, fifteen-foot pole with a wedge on the end; they would pry the abalone off a rock and pull it up with a boat hook. This practice of fishing for abalone would be outlawed in Monterey County in 1900.

By 1853, there were close to six hundred Chinese fishing the bay for everything that was out there. Villages had been established at Point Lobos, Point Alones and Mussel Point (where today the Monterey Bay Aquarium and Hopkins Marine Station are located), as well as Stillwater Cove (home of the present-day Beach & Tennis Club at Pebble Beach).

It was the foot of the abalone that Chinese were after for the most part. It was highly prized as food. It was laid out on racks to dry and sent to

China. Also, the abalone shell was sold for furniture inlay and jewelry. By 1898, the intertidal and shallower-water abalone had become scarce, and state regulations were put into place that restricted the fishing to deeper waters. Since the Chinese did not dive, those regulations ended the Chinese presence in the California abalone business.

In the nineteenth century, anti-Chinese sentiment rose to new heights in the United States; by the 1870s, no other community was so reviled as the Chinese. In 1879, a California referendum concerning Chinese immigration into the United States was placed on the ballot. Out of 5,835 votes cast in Monterey County, only 7 voted in favor of continuing Chinese immigration. On May 6, 1882, United States president Chester A. Arthur signed into law the Chinese Exclusion Act, meaning essentially that Chinese laborers were no longer allowed to immigrate to the United States. This law continued until 1943.

After the United States imposed the Chinese Exclusion Act in 1882, the number of Japanese immigrants to the West Coast increased in large numbers. One of those immigrants was a man named Otosaburo Noda, from the Saga Prefecture of Japan, who settled initially in Watsonville (about fifty miles north of Monterey) in 1895. Noda founded a lumber cutting and gathering business for the Pacific Improvement Company, the land arm of the Southern Pacific Railroad and precursor of the Pebble Beach Company. The PI Company owned about eight thousand acres of the Monterey Peninsula.

One day, while cutting wood in Monterey for the PI Company, Noda noticed the incredible variety of fish and red abalone in the Monterey Bay. Nobody was utilizing this vast marine resource. He quickly ended his lumberjack days, moved to Monterey and started a small fishing colony made up of fishermen from the Wakayama Prefecture of Japan. Noda, who would go on in 1902 to open the very first sardine cannery, Monterey Fishing & Canning Company, on what is now Cannery Row, was so taken with the Monterey area that he even wrote to the Japanese Agriculture and Commerce Department about this marine abundance. Very soon, abalone divers from the Chiba Prefecture arrived, and for the next twenty years, the Japanese dominated not only the abalone industry but also the entire fishing industry of Monterey Bay.

Chapter 2

Go West, Young Man

Almost immediately after Ernest Doelter received his naturalization papers, he moved west. His sister, Ida, having gotten married, Ernest moved to San Francisco. By the 1860s, San Francisco had more restaurants per capita than any other city in the United States besides New York. Ernest was able to obtain a job working as a waiter at a restaurant called the Cliff House. Situated on bluff overlooking the Pacific, the first Cliff House was built in 1858 from lumber salvaged from a wreck of a ship run aground on the rocks below. When Ernest arrived in San Francisco, he went to work at the third Cliff House. The second Cliff House had been severely damaged on January 16, 1887, when a schooner hauling dynamite ran aground below the Cliff House and exploded. The blast, it was said, could be heard one hundred miles away. The restaurant was quickly rebuilt. The Cliff House was a local favorite of San Francisco families, who would drive their horse-drawn carriages on a Sunday afternoon to look at the sea lions sunning themselves on the rocks near the restaurant or play in the ocean at nearby Ocean Beach and, later, swim at the nearby Sutro Baths.

Going to a restaurant in San Francisco in the late nineteenth and early twentieth centuries was more than just a meal—it was an experience. Restaurants had names like Coppas, Fashion Charlie's, the Fly Trap, Hung Far Low, the Poodle Dog, Pups, Negros and the Cob Web Palace. The Cob Web Palace was a particular favorite for children, located on the San Francisco Waterfront in a ramshackle building and filled with souvenirs and animals left from sailors who passed through. There were bears, monkeys and parrots, and everything was covered in dust and cobwebs, hence the name.

Coppas was a favorite of the bohemian crowd, who often left poetry in the guest books and on the walls of the restaurant, such as the following:

> *We may live without poetry, music and art;*
> *We may live without conscience, and live without heart;*
> *We may live without friends; we may live without books;*
> *But civilized man cannot live without cooks.*

Doelter must have visited both the Cob Web Palace and Coppas because he would later adopt many of the same ideas that made them popular. Around this time, though, he made his first trip to Monterey. When he wasn't working at the Cliff House, he was a personal chef for a wealthy San Franciscan, and together they made short trips to Monterey. Ernest fell in love with the Monterey Peninsula and vowed that he would return someday and open a restaurant.

Another probable influence on an impressionable young Ernest Doelter was a place called Woodward Gardens. Located at Mission and Thirteenth Street, Woodward Gardens was probably the first amusement park/zoo (the Cob Web Palace not withstanding) in San Francisco. Opening in 1866, it featured the first aquarium in the United States, a zoo, a roller skating rink and an art gallery. The park took up almost two full city blocks. Built by Robert B. Woodward, who made a fortune in the gold fields of California, he bought the property from the "Pathfinder," John C. Frémont, the former U.S. senator and an original signer to the California State Constitution. The park featured exotic animals like camels, llamas, alligators and ostriches. There was a live bear in a pit and a pool where you could feed the sea lions; the aquarium held octopuses and sharks, probably the first time for most people to see such animals up close. There were all kinds of entertainment for children, such as a marine life–themed merry-go-round and carts pulled by goats. There was nothing like this anywhere on the West Coast at that time. The park eventually closed in 1891, around the time that Golden Gate Park opened.

Not long after young Ernest arrived in San Francisco, he ventured out one night to the Orpheum Theater for an evening of light opera. One of the singers in the company was a beautiful young German woman named Veronica Schmolke Herrnkohl, also from Kehl, Germany. Ernest fell instantly in love. Determined to meet her, he made his way backstage and introduced himself. There must have been a mutual attraction because they were soon inseparable, so much so that when Veronica's opera company pulled up stakes for Portland, Oregon, Ernest quit his job at the Cliff House and followed. He was able to get a job as a steward (a manager) at an exclusive men's club and continued courting Veronica, who went by "Vera." They were soon married, and not long after that, their first son, Carl, named after Ernest's father, was born.

In 1891, the family moved back to San Francisco, where Ernest went to work as a steward and waiter in different restaurants around San Francisco. He also worked from time to time at the Bohemian Club, where he met and became friends with some real bohemians like California poet George Sterling and novelist Jack London. Both of these men would play a future role in making Ernest and his abalone steak famous.

It wasn't long before Carl had a baby brother named Ernest Jr. and then a sister named Vera. With a growing family, Doelter needed to find a more secure and better-paying job. In 1895, the new Pacific Yacht Club opened in Sausalito, and Ernest got the job as the chief steward. This position also included living quarters. The club opened to the public

The Pacific Yacht Club. "Pop" was the steward for the Pacific Yacht Club in Sausalito and can be seen in this photo sitting in the middle of the front row with his right hand on his knee. Circa 1895. *Author's collection.*

on May 12, 1895; this is how the *San Francisco Call Bulletin* described the opening: "Steward Ernest Doelter looked after the inner man and inner woman, and set up a most sumptuous repast. Everybody lingered over the steward's table until the red fire began to glow and the Chinese and Japanese lanterns began to dance in the rigging of the craft."

The good times didn't last long. Just one month later, Doelter had to let go a Japanese waiter (whose name is now lost to history) because he was living outside on the grounds and building small campfires too close the boathouse, where the wooden boats were kept. The waiter had been warned not to do this, but he continued to camp and build his fires on the grounds. On the morning of June 26, 1895, Doelter paid the waiter his final wages and told him to leave the grounds. Before leaving, the former waiter turned and threatened Doelter, saying, "I will see you again." Right before noon, he returned with a small .22-caliber revolver hidden in his pocket. Sneaking through the gate and entering the Doelter family home without being seen, he made his way to the second floor of the house, where the children were taking a nap in their rooms, and hid in a bathroom and waited.

Around this same time, Ernest and Vera were sitting down for lunch. Before they could finish, one of the children woke up and began to fuss. Mrs. Doelter immediately went upstairs to tend to her child. As she was passing the bathroom, the discharged waiter jumped out and shot her, the bullet striking her right shoulder. Vera screamed and ran to the children's room as another shot was fired, missing her and hitting the wall next to the room. Upon hearing the first gunshot, Ernest ran up the stairs, meeting the would-be assassin in the hallway and charging him. The gunman fired at Ernest, just barely missing him. Ernest, who was a big man standing over six feet, tackled the man and wrestled him to the ground, taking control of the gun. Others on the yacht club grounds heard all the commotion and went to investigate, arriving at the scene just in time to help Doelter tie the man up. The police were called, and the man was arrested. A doctor was also called. Luckily, Mrs. Doelter was not seriously injured, and she recovered within a few days—at least from the gunshot wounds. Not long after the shooting, the Doelter family left the Pacific Yacht Club and moved to a new business venture on the outskirts of the city of San Francisco called the Trocadero.

Chapter 3
Diving Abalone

A round the time that the Doelters were packing their bags to move from the yacht club, Otosaburo Noda was in Monterey developing a small Japanese fishing colony on what is now present-day Cannery Row. Along with the ten fishermen from Wakayama Prefecture, and two men named Kanno and Imajo (first names unknown) who came with him from Watsonville, Noda also partnered with Hyakutaro Ide from Shizuoka Prefecture, who supplied all the food for the colony.

Early in 1896, Noda and Hyakutaro Ide contacted a business associate in Japan named Shoya Isobe, informing him of the great potential for abalone in Monterey. Isobe asked the Japanese Ministry of Agriculture and Commerce to help find an expert who could develop an abalone fishery in California. They suggested Gennosuke Kodani, who was in the abalone business on the Boso Peninsula in the Chiba Prefecture. Kodani received his first passport to California/Monterey on September 9, 1897. One month later, Gennosuke Kodani arrived in Monterey. In early December 1897, three divers—Ichinosuke Yasuda, Daisuke Yasuda and Rinji Yamamoto—along with Gennosuke Kodani's younger brother, Nakajiro, a trained marine biologist, arrived at the train station in Monterey. The men were picked up and taken to Noda's fishing colony about two miles away. The very next day, they were diving for abalone in Monterey Bay. These first three divers were *ama*, or free-divers. Dressed in a thin, two-piece white cotton outfit, with an abalone basket (a netted bag), an abalone pry and a pair of goggles (which had pigs' bladders attached to either side that the diver could

Above: Abalone dive crew at Point Lobos. Gennosuke Kodani is the fourth man from the left, with his hands in his pockets. Note the diver standing on the ladder. Circa 1900. *Kodani Family Collection.*

Left: Otosaburo Noda (foreground) and Gennosuke Kodani in Monterey. Circa 1900. *City of Monterey, California History Room.*

squeeze to help release the pressure), these men swam into the cold waters of the Monterey Bay resting on small rounded wooden floats called *ukidaru* (*uki* means "floating" and *daru* means "wooden barrel").

The divers could stay underwater for up to two minutes gathering abalone. The water temperature in Monterey Bay is about fifteen degrees colder than in Japan—a big difference.

Kodani began to look for a suitable place that was close to the Monterey Harbor yet far enough away from the town that he could be left relatively alone to build his abalone business. He stumbled onto Point Lobos, about five miles south of Carmel, one afternoon and met the owner, Alexander MacMillan Allan. Allan was a pretty progressive thinker for his time. Among other things, he was mining engineer who came to Point Lobos to run a coal mine. At the time that he bought the property, Point Lobos had been subdivided for large housing community. Allan bought all the lots that had already been sold and essentially preserved it.

Kodani immediately saw the possibilities for his abalone business at Point Lobos. He talked to Allan, who liked what he heard, and the two became partners. Besides building a cannery and housing, including a traditional Japanese-style bath, for his

Alexander MacMillan Allan, Gennosuke Kodani's partner and owner of Point Lobos. Allan was a mining engineer who first came to the Monterey Peninsula to run a coal mine at Point Lobos. He eventually bought the property and preserved it. He also ran a sardine cannery, Monterey Fish Company, on present-day Cannery Row. Circa 1895. *Kodani Family Collection.*

divers, Kodani also sent for helmet divers. Helmet diving was much more efficient than old-school *ama* diving. The diver could stay down for hours at a time gathering abalone. Helmet diving in Japan was pretty new technology then, but entire industries in Japan were developed just for it. Companies in Tokyo were making diving gear to support this new method of diving.

To help with the cold Monterey Bay, the divers learned to knit. They would take wool sweaters, tear them apart and knit woolen underwear, kind of like long johns. Eventually, these dive gear companies in Tokyo began to make this kind of underwear just for the California Japanese abalone fishery. The divers would put on these two-piece items called "woolies," sometimes

Logo for the Point Lobos Canning Company. Circa 1900. *Kodani Family Collection.*

Two abalone dive boats at Point Lobos. The boats were converted whaling boats. The man on the right holding the rope is a Portuguese whaler. Note the buildings in the background, part of the compound for the Japanese crew, including a bunkhouse and a traditional Japanese bath. Circa 1899. *Kodani Family Collection.*

two pairs; put on heavy canvas suits; attach about sixty-five pounds of lead weights to their fronts and backs; tie lead to their shoes; bolt on the thirty-pound helmets, which had hoses attached to them; and then descend into the bay.

Initially, the boats were equipped with a hand pump, and two to four men would hand-pump the air to the diver. The diver would descend to about thirty feet. The deeper he went, the harder it was to pump. He would be down all day collecting abalone. These pumps had to be taken apart and lubricated with oil every day. The only high-quality oil that could be found around Monterey was olive oil, which was perfect for lubricating the pumps. The problem was that the divers would complain that all they could smell for the first hour was olive oil. Ishimatsu Kurihara, Sennosuke Hayakawa and Jiromatsu Yamaguchi, the first helmet divers, arrived in Monterey from the Boso Peninsula sometime in October 1898. They were taken out to Point Lobos, and once again, they were helmet diving for abalone the very next day.

Even though helmet diving was more efficient—and warmer—there were still companies in Monterey that dove in traditional *ama* style. Working in

Two early *ama* divers at Point Lobos. Note the goggles. Circa 1898. *Kodani Family Collection.*

pairs, one diver would go down, following the anchor line from the boat. He would collect as much abalone has he could in two minutes, putting the abalone in his basket. When it was time for the *ama* to return to the surface, his partner on the boat would throw a large rock over the side that was tied to a rope and threaded through a pulley system. The other end of that rope was tied around the diver's waist, pulling the *ama* to the surface quickly. As soon as the *ama* hit the surface, his partner dove in. The first diver made his way onto the boat, where he would warm up next a fire burning in a barrel on the boat. In 1907, there was a Japanese report concerning the treatment of Japanese citizens in California; it noted in 1902 that one Monterey abalone company employed female divers from the Shizuoka Prefecture to harvest abalone.

Chapter 4

The Trocadero

When the Doelter family took over the Trocadero, it had only been open for about four years. Built by a man named George M. Greene, whose family began homesteading the property in 1847, the Trocadero consisted of a small hotel surrounded by cabins and a lake that was fully stocked with rainbow trout. The lake was considered to be the best fishing lake in all of Northern California. It also had a park for hunting deer. The Trocadero was *the* spot—the rendezvous of the San Francisco elite on the weekends. At that time, the area was pretty remote. It was like going out into the country. When Ernest became the proprietor, he added a dancing pavilion and a traditional beer garden that poured German-style beer in steins. He also brought dogs, parrots, goats, monkeys and even a large brown bear that he kept in a pit. The family moved into one of the larger cabins on the property, and business at the Trocadero was good. The hotel and cabins were full almost every weekend and oftentimes during the week. Ernest was a gracious host, always tending to his guests' every need, and the animals were a popular attraction.

The bear would be fed every afternoon at 5:00 p.m., and a big show would be made of it. Ernest would put a ladder into the pit and climb down with a large hunk of meat, which he would leave at the bottom of the pit for the bear. One day in February 1896, after feeding the bear and climbing out of the pit, he forgot to remove the ladder. The bear, after eating his dinner, managed to climb the ladder and escape his prison. The Doelter children were playing nearby and saw the bear approach.

They panicked and screamed, getting the attention of the family dogs, which proceeded to chase the frightened bear into the woods. A number of guests also saw the bear and picked up sticks and rocks to throw at the poor retreating animal.

Doelter was dismayed at the thought of losing this expensive attraction. It took a few hours, but eventually he was able recover the terrified bear and returned him to his pit. This was such a big story that it made the *San Francisco Chronicle* the next day. The story made its way across the country, and each time it was published, the story got bigger. By the time it reached the *Omaha Evening World-Herald* about a year later, the bear had been chained to a tree, broke the chain and made its way into the Doelter family home. After napping in the master bedroom, the bear found the children playing in an adjacent room, where the bear batted young Carl Doelter around like a ping-pong ball. Ernest appeared with his bulldog and a shotgun and chased the bear into the nearby woods, where he caught up to it and shot it dead!

Not long after the bear incident, the Doelters welcomed their newest member to the family, daughter Minnie. Just about a year later, in April 1897, another occurrence happened that put Doelter in the news again. Throughout his life, Doelter was always looking for new and different ways to market his business. In the late 1890s, the United States was suffering from a depression, and as a consequence, there were a great number of unemployed men. A plan was hatched by the San Francisco business community to help these men. The plan was to employ these men to build a road from downtown San Francisco all the way out to the boulevards, where there were no roads. This included going right past the Trocadero.

Monies were raised and the work began, employing close to seven hundred men. As the work progressed and got closer to the Trocadero, Ernest wanted to show his gratitude to these hardworking men and had the idea of putting on a barbecue for the workers right in front of his establishment. This idea did not sit well with the downtown business community. Owners felt that Ernest was doing this as an advertising scheme to promote the Trocadero. On April 5, the day before the planned barbecue, a phone call was placed to Doelter to tell him to halt his plans, but he never got the message. It was too late by then anyway; he had already dug a pit, started a fire, placed some iron bars across the pit and put on a "quartered bullock" to roast the whole night. On the morning of April 6, as the bullock was still roasting, Ernest and his assistants set up tables and put out potatoes, bread and hardboiled eggs for the hungry road workers. He even had wagons ready to take food to the workers who were too far down the line. The merchants were not happy! They felt that the only way to stop it was to absolutely forbid any man from partaking in this feast. If one did, he would be immediately discharged and have his work ticket taken from him.

The superintendent overseeing the project was a man named Mr. Eagan, and it was his job to ride up down the line informing the workers of this new edict. Of course, word got out to the workers of this free lunch, and many hadn't brought a meal that day. This did not sit well with them. They could already smell the appetizing aroma coming from Doelters' barbecue pit.

When Ernest was informed of the merchants' plan, he was not pleased either. He told Eagan "that he had no designs in the matter except to give the men a good hot dinner. They were hardly of the class that frequented his place, and he could not expect to make profit out of it!"

The hungry workers were getting boisterous, and there some concern that there might be a riot. The police were called, and the press arrived.

Feeding the unemployed. This drawing appeared in the *San Francisco Call* on April 7, 1897. It shows Pop standing over a barbecue pit preparing a meal for a group of very hungry road workers. This is the first time that his image had ever appeared in any kind of publication. Circa 1897.

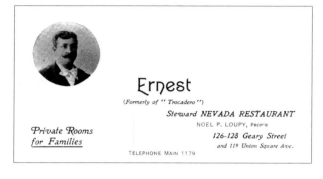

Ernest

(Formerly of "Trocadero")

Steward NEVADA RESTAURANT

NOEL P. LOUPY, PROP'R

Private Rooms for Families

126-128 Geary Street

and 119 Union Square Ave.

TELEPHONE MAIN 1179

Business card for the Nevada Restaurant. After Pop left the Trocadero, he briefly worked at the Nevada Restaurant in San Francisco. Note the wonderful photo of Pop and the one name, "Ernest." Circa 1898. *Pat Sands Collection.*

When Eagan approached the unruly workers, one of them raised his hat and stepped in front of Eagan and said:

> *"If you fellows are afraid I am not. I am going to show my independence. I am going to eat. Eagan, come and take lunch with me." He went straight into the chained circle in the center of which stood Doelter, coat off and sleeve rolled up hard at work, and in a few minutes returned with a heaped plate into the doleful circle of his fellow workers to add to their temptation. Only one or two followed his example, however, the others stoically refusing to fall.*

That's how the *San Francisco Call* reported the scene the next day. There was also a drawing of Ernest Doelter over his barbecue pit accompanying the article. The workers who got Ernest's lunch lost their jobs but went home happy and full. The rest picked up their shovels and wheelbarrows and went back to work hungry. Doelter and his crew gathered up all the remaining food and carted it away.

The Doelters continued to run the Trocadero for a few more years, after which it was taken over by man named C.A. Hooper, a wealthy lumberman.

In about 1900, the family moved to San Francisco proper, where Ernest got a job as the headwaiter at the Nevada Restaurant. Located on Pine Street, the Nevada was known for its more simple American fare, like roast beef. He also opened a liquor shop on Folsom Street and continued working at the Bohemian Club. The family also welcomed Otto, their newest son, into the fold.

Chapter 5

Abalone in Monterey

While Doelter was establishing himself in San Francisco, the Japanese in Monterey were diving for abalone. Because there was no real market in Monterey (or California, for that matter) for abalone, the Japanese companies were drying it and shipping it back to Japan. They were also shipping it to China, Hawaii and Australia, where there were large Japanese and Chinese communities that would buy it. There was also a great deal of anti-Japanese sentiment in the United States at that time, coming mainly from white workers who were convinced that the Japanese were coming to take their jobs.

So, after a few years of watching all this dried abalone being shipped from the Monterey Wharf, a number of the local citizens in Monterey created a petition drive to try to stop the Japanese from gathering any more abalone. Their concern was that the Japanese would take it all—not that the good citizens of Monterey really wanted it. There was also a concern that it would hurt the tourist trade. Many visitors to Monterey had never seen abalone before, and they would often take the shells home as a souvenir. At that time, many of the divers were creating abalone jewelry, like brooches and pins or watch fobs for the men, which they were selling to the tourists to make extra money.

In October 1899, a meeting of the Monterey County Board of Supervisors was convened to discuss the abalone issue. The Japanese abalone industry was well represented at the meeting. Nakajiro Kodani, the younger brother of Gennosuke Kodani and a trained marine biologist, showed the supervisors that they were only taking the large and older abalone and leaving the young and smaller abalone so they could reproduce. They felt that if the larger abalone were

Point Lobos Abalone Company boats going out for a dive. The dive boat is being pulled by the boat with the American flag. You can see the dive suit draped over the side of the dive boat. Circa 1900. *Kodani Family Collection.*

left alone, they would die of old age and "be lost to the world." Kodani added, "The abalone is naturally given to us and we should make a profit of it; if we leave them alone at the bottom of the sea we are acting against the will of God."

The supervisors eventually ruled that the Japanese could not dive for abalone north of the Carmel River and that the divers had to pay a sixty-dollar fishing license fee every year.

OAK PARK AND THE GRAND CENTRAL HOTEL

In 1903, the Doelter family packed up and moved again, this time to Stockton, California, about sixty-five miles northeast of San Francisco, where Ernest took over a place called Oak Park. Very similar to the Trocadero, Oak Park had cabins, a dancing pavilion, a fully stocked fishing lake and a beer garden. He also brought all of his animals, including the bear. Oak Park was advertised as the "Finest Picnic and Recreation grounds in the State." Doelter was trying to attract the

Business card for Oak Park in Stockton. It had a fully stocked fishing lake, a beer garden and a petting zoo. Circa 1903. *Pat Sands Collection.*

The young Doelter family in the backyard of the their Capp Street home in San Francisco. *From left to right, sitting*: Vera, Minnie, Otto, Ernest Jr. and Carl. Mother Veronica is standing behind, on the stairs. Circa 1901. *Pat Sands Collection.*

The 1906
The
Central Hotel
Large Sunny Rooms

Leading Hotel in Gilroy.
Excellent Cuisine

DRUMMERS' HEADQUARTERS
Commodious Sample Rooms

E. Doelter, Prop.
Gilroy, Cal.

Business card for the Central Hotel Gilroy. Pop gave up running the hotel and moved to Monterey when the City of Gilroy raised his liquor license fee. Circa 1906. *Pat Sands Collection.*

same San Francisco crowd that would visit the Trocadero—he advertised "Extremely Low Rates between San Francisco and Stockton by Santa FE R.R. Time, 2 hours and 20 minutes." It's not known how many San Franciscans actually visited Oak Park or how good (or bad) business actually was. It is also not known if there were any bear escapades, but in 1906, the family moved once again. This time to Gilroy, about 105 miles south, to take over the Grand Central Hotel. The bear did not make the trip.

The Grand Central Hotel was on an old stagecoach line near the rail line south of San Jose and a hot springs. It was a large hotel with a restaurant and saloon. It was popular with folks visiting the hot springs. Doelter would travel by train to Monterey (about fifty miles south) from time to time to pick up special supplies for the hotel. While in Monterey, he stayed at the St. Charles Hotel, where he became close friends with the proprietor, Charley Casper.

By the turn of the twentieth century, the temperance movement in the United States had gained steam. Pressure was being placed on communities to eliminate—or, at the very least, reduce the number of—liquor shops and saloons in their towns. Gilroy was no different. On January 7, 1907, the Gilroy Town Council voted to raise the liquor license fees from $300 per year to $1,000 per year. Ernest Doelter, who attended the meeting, was vehemently against this new ordinance, as he relied on the business of his saloon. He was listed in the local newspaper as one of the leaders of the opposition. The *San Jose Mercury News* headline for January 8 read, "Gilroy Saloons Given Death Blow!" Although the new ordinance wouldn't take effect until July, Ernest began looking for a new venture, setting his sights on Monterey.

Chapter 6

Canned Abalone and Monterey

S hipping dried abalone across the Pacific isn't as easy as it may sound. There were inherent problems. The dried abalone was packed in burlap sacks and stowed in the holds of ships. It was not uncommon for the ships to take on water, flooding the holds and drenching the burlap sacks, thus spoiling the whole shipment of abalone before it reached its intended destination. This could be a financial disaster. So, the Japanese abalone companies began to look for new ways to preserve their product.

At the turn of the twentieth century, the Monterey sardine industry was in its infancy. At that time, all the sardines were cooked in hot oil, olive oil or peanut oil, which was called the "French method," a slow and sometimes dangerous process. All the sardines had to be dried before cooking so they wouldn't spatter when put into the hot oil and cause a fire. Everything was done by hand.

At this same time, in San Pedro California, a tuna processor named Albert P. Halfhill was looking for a new way to cook his tuna. In those days, people didn't eat tuna like we do today. They said it had a "funny taste to it." He finally came up with the idea of steaming the tuna in the can. He was so happy with this process, and so happy with the taste of his canned tuna, that he traveled up and down California promoting his "Chicken of the Sea" tuna. The Monterey canneries quickly adapted this new steamed process—it was faster and cleaner, and there was a better taste to the product.

When Gennosuke Kodani and A.M. Allan built a cannery out at Point Lobos, they also began to can their abalone using this new steam process.

Above: Inside the Point Lobos Cannery. You can see the boilers behind the unidentified man with the clipboard. Circa 1920. *Kodani Family Collection.*

Left: Gennosuke Kodani sitting in a pile of large red abalone shells at Point Lobos. Note the Point Lobos Cannery behind him. Circa 1930. *Kodani Family Collection.*

MONTEREY

On June 11, the *San Jose Mercury News* reported, "Ernest Doelter returned last evening from a business trip to Monterey where he may locate in business after the first of July." Ever since that first visit, Ernest had always wanted to move to Monterey, and with the city of Gilroy's new higher liquor license fee taking effect, this was his time.

In early July 1907, the family once again packed up all their belongings, including their animals, and boarded the Southern Pacific's Del Monte Express bound for Monterey. It was just a short walk from the train station to the St. Charles Hotel, where the family would be staying until they could find a more permanent place to live. Also, right behind the St. Charles, at 441 Alvarado Street, was the new restaurant building that Ernest had just taken over. The building was owned by Thomas Albert Work, known around Monterey as T.A. Work, a businessman and banker who owned a lot of property around the Monterey Peninsula. Having emigrated from Scotland in 1883, his grandfather was a sea captain who had sailed the California coast in the mid-nineteenth century and told Thomas that Monterey was one of the most beautiful places in the world. T.A. worked a variety of different jobs when he first came to the Monterey area, including delivering milk and selling firewood. He opened a grain and feed store, and in 1900, he became a partner in the First National Bank of Monterey, eventually becoming the full owner of the bank in 1906.

Renamed Café Ernest, Doelter's small restaurant, which had a seating capacity for about twenty, featured "Toke Point Oysters." Oysters were a very desirable food item at that time, and Toke Point or blue oysters were considered the very best. These were transplanted oysters from the East Coast. Although the Pacific oyster, a local oyster, was easily available, restaurants in San Francisco preferred their East Coast cousin. The Toke Point was raised in oyster beds all over San Francisco Bay, and Ernest had them shipped by train on ice. He would place simple ads in the local newspaper like, "Café Ernest. Taste Will Tell."

Advertisement for the Café Ernest before Pop discovered the abalone. Circa 1907. *Author's collection.*

CELEBRATED
"Toke Point" Oysters
Cafe Ernest
Stew or Fry 30c.
441 ALVARADO ST.

He also counted on guests from the Hotel Del Monte to eat at the restaurant. The hotel opened in June 1880 and was a railroad hotel, built by Charles Crocker, one of the "Big Four" owners of the Southern Pacific. The railroad first came to Monterey in 1874 as a locally owned line called the Monterey Salinas Valley Railroad. This small railroad was built in order to ship fish to San Francisco and vegetables from the Salinas Valley, as well as to attract tourism to the Monterey area. It was not financially successful. The Monterey Salinas Valley Railroad was bought out in 1880 by the Southern Pacific. When the SP bought the MSVR, it also bought about eight thousand acres of the Monterey Peninsula with the idea of turning Monterey into a tourist attraction.

With all these potential tourists, you need a place for them to stay. So the rail company built the Hotel Del Monte on 126 acres in just three months. It was the first resort in the United States, often advertised as "The Most Elegant Seaside Resort in the World" or "California's Largest and Best Loved Resort." The hotel was called a "winter hotel," The Del Monte would be marketed to wealthy families who lived on the East Coast to get out of those cold winters and spend a few months at the Hotel Del Monte. It had beautiful gardens designed by the famed landscape architect Rudolph Ulrich. There was a racetrack, art galleries, polo, sport fishing on the Monterey Bay and, of course, golf. It also created the famed seventeen-mile drive. The hotel hosted presidents and royalty in what was then the most beautiful hotel in the world.

Since all the Doelter children called their father "Pop," it didn't take long before everyone in Monterey called him "Pop" as well. The Café Ernest became a popular place, and the whole family worked in the restaurant. Ernest Doelter Jr., who was fifteen at the time, worked as a cook, along with Pop, while his younger brother Carl, age seventeen, and mother, Vera, worked the dining room. Young Vera, fourteen, acted as the cashier. The two younger children, Minnie, ten, and Otto, seven, also worked in the restaurant. For a short time, the Doelter family lived in the restaurant building until they found a home on what was then Main Street (now Calle Principal) just a few blocks from the restaurant. Because most of their business was a dinner crowd, the kids went to school during the day and worked at the restaurant at night.

Chapter 7

The Bohemians

A few years before the Doelter family moved to Monterey, the California poet and bohemian George Sterling and his wife, Carrie, moved south from the hustle and bustle of the San Francisco Bay area to the solitude of Carmel by the Sea. It didn't take long for other artists, poets and writers—like Mary Austin; poet Nora May French; writers James Hopper, Sinclair Lewis, Upton Sinclair and John Hilliard; photographer Arnold Genthe; Xavier Martinez; and, from time to time, Jack London—to follow, creating an artist's colony in Carmel, where George Sterling was crowned "King Bohemian."

These bohemians would hold picnics at Carmel Beach, gathering abalone from the intertidal at low tide. Removing them from the shell, they would pound them to tenderize them, cut them up into small bite-sized pieces and then place the abalone into water in a small black cast-iron pot that was cooking over an open fire on the beach. They would also add vegetables, carrots and potatoes and sometimes other meats to the pot to create a kind of abalone stew.

It wasn't long after Doelter opened his restaurant in Monterey that he also began work as a caterer. His catering business was successful, and when he was not working in the restaurant, he was catering some event around Monterey. One such event in late January 1908 was a banquet he catered at Colton Hall (built by Walter Colton in 1846 and where the California Constitution was drafted in the fall of 1849) for the Eagle and Bear, two fraternal organizations. According to the *Monterey Daily Cypress*, "It was a joyful occasion at which the best of cheer prevailed. The menu was an elaborate one, the toasts were sharp and witty, and the two organizations met in fellowship that tends to the betterment of a community and mankind." The *Cypress* went on to note, "Ernest Doelter of the Café Ernest was caterer and the banquet was a credit to him." This was the menu as published in the *Cypress* on January 23, 1908:

SALAD
Sauterne Crab Salad, Eagles Claws

SOUP
Consommé au Tass, Bear Paw

FISH
Filet of Sole   Sauce Tarter
Ricolly Potatoes, Eagle Valley
Zinfandel

COLD ROAST MEATS
Turkey, Bear Flat, Tongue, Eagle
Hafa Kingan, Grizzly
Pickles, Olives

DESSERT
Fruit, Cheese, Café Noir
Pineapple Sherbet

He clearly catered his menu to his patrons.

Another big event that same year was the arrival of the Atlantic Fleet on May 1, 1908. Conceived by President Theodore Roosevelt in 1907 as a way to show the world that the United States military power was a force to be reckoned with, this around-the-world trip of sixteen battleships nicknamed the "Great White Fleet" because the hulls of the ships were painted white. The fleet set sail from Hampton Roads, Virginia, on December 16, 1907.

By 1906, anti-Japanese sentiment in California was rampant. In San Francisco, the board of education decided to segregate all Japanese schoolchildren. The board's decision did not sit well with the citizens of Japan, and there were violent anti-American protests in the streets of Tokyo. In the United States, members of the anti-Japanese movement felt that these protests in Tokyo were being inflamed by the Japanese in

"The Bohemians." *Tom Fordham Collection.*

California. Otosaburo Noda, who had sold his Monterey cannery in 1907, traveled to Washington, D.C., to speak to the Japanese consul general on behalf of the Japanese citizens of California. Many in the anti-Japanese movement were convinced that Noda was trying to provoke a war between Japan and the United States. After his trip to Washington, D.C., Noda returned to Monterey, where he was interviewed by the *Monterey Daily Cypress* about his trip. He told the paper, "I am not leading a movement that is plotting the overthrow of the government." He went on to say, "It is true I went to Washington as the representative of the Japanese residents of California. Ever since the controversy over the school question in San Francisco there has been all kinds of rumors of strained relations between the two governments. The Japanese of this State heard all the rumors and they became restless. So it was decided I should go on to Washington and set things straight and find out what was being done."

Besides meeting the Japanese consul general, he also met with President Roosevelt, for whom he put on a sumo wrestling contest in the East Room of the White House. As it happened, there was a traveling sumo team on an international tour that was in the Washington, D.C. area at the time. Noda contacted the team and arranged the demonstration in the White House.

Roosevelt was able to make an agreement with Japan that would restrict the numbers of Japanese immigrants coming into the United States. Called the "Gentlemen's Agreement," Japan agreed to not issue passports to laborers coming to the United States. In exchange, the San Francisco Board of Education would end its segregationist policy against Japanese schoolchildren. This Gentlemen's Agreement had severe repercussions for the Monterey/California abalone industry because divers were no longer allowed to immigrate. It would be more than ten years before another diver from Japan could come to work in the United States.

Roosevelt was still concerned about Japanese retaliation, and he did not want to go to war with Japan. So, he sent his Atlantic Fleet on its around-the-world trip that would eventually sail into Tokyo Bay. After the fleet left Virginia, it made its way through the Caribbean, around South America and Mexico and up the California Coast, finally arriving in Monterey.

The city of Monterey went from a population of 6,000 to 100,000 in one day. People came from all over to see the Great White Fleet. And what a sight it was! The streets of Monterey were filled with sailors and tourists, and over the next week, there were parties, dances, parades and baseball games. And the Café Ernest was going to be right in the middle of all this celebration. Earlier that spring, when it was announced that the fleet would visit Monterey, Ernest took over 443 Alvarado Street, the store right next door to his restaurant, and he was able to expand from twenty seats to more than sixty. The Café Ernest and "annex" were full of hungry customers every day of the fleet's visit.

It was also around this time that Ernest began to have shipment problems. His Toke Point oysters didn't always arrive fresh from San Francisco, and a fresh product was always important to Doelter. Oftentimes the trains would be delayed, making their arrival into Monterey sometimes hours late. Of course, the ice that was keeping the oysters fresh would have melted, spoiling the whole shipment.

He began to look for a local product to replace the oysters. Mussels were easily available, but he wanted something new, something special, and abalone was his ticket. Abalone itself wasn't particularly new. On May 28, 1892, the *Pacific Rural Press* published K.P.S. Boyd's article "At Pacific Grove," which noted, "One would not eat in the kitchen, but one might, on occasion, cook in the dining-room, especially if, as to-day, one had a fresh abalone (Haliotis—'ear of the sea') to chop and boil until perfectly tender, with a little pork and potato, for our delicious soup, tasting very like, but much nicer, than clam stew."

Interior of the Café Ernest on Alvarado Street in downtown Monterey. Circa 1907. *Pat Sands Collection.*

By the turn of the twentieth century, it was also appearing on menus in Monterey, typically at banquets or special events. The usual method of cooking abalone then was to boil it in vinegar or bake it, often using lye to tenderize it. When the canned product became available, restaurants would make a salad or soup out of it. By 1908, many of the upscale restaurants in San Francisco and Los Angeles were serving abalone chowder, all from the canned product. Unfortunately, it's not known exactly when (or, for that matter, where) Pop got the idea to start cooking abalone. He certainly would have seen it and probably utilized it at some of the banquets he catered. He was also being pushed into a new direction because newer restaurants were opening in Monterey, each offering something new and special.

He was going to make an abalone steak, something no one else was doing or had even thought of at that time. Doelter believed that he could make it palatable and appetizing without boiling or using lye. Many of the chefs in Monterey thought he was foolhardy and told him that it couldn't be done. He brought the abalone into his restaurant one day and began to experiment.

THE ABALONE KING OF MONTEREY

Being German, he was, of course, very familiar with *wiener schnitzel*, a lightly pounded veal cutlet that's coated in flour and cracker crumbs, run through an egg wash and then cooked in oil or lard. This seemed to work very well with the abalone. Ernest would slice off the foot to make a steak and pound it four or five times with a wooden mallet or a rolling pin (the pounding breaks up the connective tissues, making the abalone tender). He seasoned it with salt and pepper and then added his secret ingredient, "abalone nectar" (the juice that came out of the shell). He ran the abalone steak through an egg wash, added cracker crumbs and cooked it up quickly in olive oil or butter. In another version of this recipe, he would, after seasoning with salt and pepper and abalone nectar, cook the abalone without the egg wash and cracker crumbs. He also made an abalone soup using the nectar as the base, as well as abalone chowder and stew.

Word got out very quickly about this new seafood sensation, and the Café Ernest became the hot spot in Northern California. People came from all over to eat Pop's fresh abalone steaks. Business became so good that he had to hire extra help, including a young man named Walter Stokes, a Monterey native whose family first came to the peninsula in the early 1830s. Walter eventually married daughter Vera.

Everyone wanted to know his secret for tenderizing the abalone, but Doelter was tight-lipped. One chef was convinced that the tenderizing happened because of the method Doelter used to kill the abalone. The chef was so convinced that he approached Doelter's young daughter Mimi, hoping to get the secret out of her. After making the chef swear to an oath of secrecy, she told him, "Pop strangles them."

Joseph and Edward Gayetty—two brothers from the San Francisco Bay area who had the first abalone business in Monterey in the 1890s and now were running a new abalone cannery in Cayucos, San Luis Obispo County, in 1909—believed that "if the abalone is killed by electricity its flesh is rendered soft and succulent, like that of an oyster."

In 1909, Doelter turned his "annex" at 443 Alvarado Street into a beer tavern called Ernest's Tavern. The *Monterey Daily Cypress* wrote of this new endeavor on September 30, 1909, "The Ernest Tavern will be a place unique in Monterey. Besides a bar that will be supplied with all the choicest liquors, there will be a kitchen in the rear where everything in the market can be secured. There will be tables where parties can sit down and pass a social hour over a properly cooked meal and a glass of beer, wine or ale. A first class restaurant known as Ernest Café adjoins the Tavern and will be conducted along the lines that it has heretofore."

Beer was important to Pop as well. All beer served up in his tavern was the finest and the freshest and always came in a German beer stein. He also became the sole agent for the Wunder Beer Company. The first Wunder Beer brewer was a man named John C. Wunder, a German immigrant who founded the San Diego Brewing Company in San Francisco in 1896. He then bought another San Francisco brewery, Bavaria Brewing, in 1898 and combined the two to become Wunder Beer. This was around the same that Doelter was running the Trocadero, so he probably knew John Wunder and had served Wunder Beer at his beer garden. Later, after leaving the Trocadero, Doelter sold it at his liquor store. The original Wunder Brewery was destroyed on April 18, 1906, in the San Francisco earthquake and fire. It's not known if John C. Wunder was involved in this new endeavor in Monterey, but you could go into the Ernest Tavern and buy a stein of Wunder Beer for about five cents.

In the early days of the Monterey sardine fishery, the fishermen would use bottles to float their nets. Special bottles were made with a round bottom, so they could not stand upright. In those days, if you put a

Pop was always willing to have his picture taken with his customers. Here he is with two unknown ladies in front of his restaurant at the foot of the Monterey Wharf. Circa 1925. *Pat Sands Collection.*

carbonated beverage in an upright bottle, the carbonation would pop the cork, but if it were on its side, it didn't have that problem. The bottles were filled with beer, probably Wunder from Ernest Tavern, and used to float their nets in the cold water of the Monterey Bay. When they were done fishing, they pulled in the floats, and everyone had cold beer.

Ever since the shooting incident with his wife, Vera, at the Pacific Yacht Club, Doelter had been a little apprehensive working with the Japanese community. But in order to get abalone for the restaurant, he had to learn to work with them.

Pop initially got his abalone from different Japanese sources at the Monterey Wharf. He eventually went to Kodani and Allan's Monterey Abalone Company at Point Lobos for all of his abalone needs. He became friends with both men, and the three created a symbiotic relationship that would last for the rest of their lives. He also hired Tomekichi Manaka, a Japanese immigrant, to work as a cook in the restaurant. The Manakas were one of the pioneering fishing families in Monterey.

The Japanese Monterey abalone industry was a colorful one. People would go down to the wharf or along the Monterey waterfront to watch the *ama* work. At the 1909 Fourth of July celebration, a Monterey merchant named Manuel Duarte (the Duarte family owned a number of businesses

The Point Lobos Canning Company. Circa 1917. *Kodani Family Collection.*

Early *ama* divers at Point Lobos. Note the diver with the rockfish at the end of his spear. Circa 1900. *Kodani Family Collection.*

along the Monterey waterfront that catered to the tourist trade, including fish markets and a "Marine Museum") had scheduled special glass-bottom boat rides on his "Venetian Gondola," *El Buso* (in Spanish, "el buso" means "the diver"). For twenty-five cents, he promised that patrons would see beautiful "Marine Gardens…A large submarine sandbank, where you see thousands of Clams, with varieties of Star Fish of various colors. Then enter another garden different entirely from the first. Then over skeletons of Whales at the bottom of the bay with hundreds on Abalones on them… Words cannot describe or give credit to the wonderful sight until you see it with your own eyes." And for an extra fifty cents, "I have also engaged the celebrated Japanese Diver Kse Ko who will dive from the boat in his native costume and get anything the passenger may desire. Also when in action at the bottom of the bay will place the glass over him and you get a good view of his wonderful work and endurance."

Of course, the Café Ernest became a favorite for all those bohemians, and they would often come to eat fresh abalone steaks. They also would leave short abalone ditties or poetry in the Café Ernest guest book, which would encourage others to do the same. Now known as the "Abalone Song," these original verses predate the Café Ernest. Those early bohemians, while preparing their abalone on Carmel Beach, would write these ditties, such as:

> *Oh! some folks boast of quail on toast*
> *Because they think it's tony;*
> *But I'm content to owe my rent*
> *And live on abalone.*

That particular verse, considered to be the opening verse to the song, was written in the Café Ernst guest book on August 30, 1913, by George Sterling. Rather, Sterling has always gotten credit for writing this verse, but in fact, it was probably written several years earlier by Opal Heron Search, a talented musician and local actress who lived in Carmel. Although it's not believed that Jack London wrote any of the abalone song verses, he was the first to include many of the verses in his book *The Valley of the Moon*, published in September 1913. In the novel, the character Mark Hall (based on Sterling) tells Billy (based on Jack London), "You must never, never pound abalone without singing this song. Nor must you sing this song at any other time. It would be the rankest sacrilege."

George Sterling wrote out his final version of the abalone song in 1920 and had it printed to give out to friends:

> *Oh! Some folks boast of quail and toast,*
> *Because they think it's tony;*
> *But I'm content to owe my rent*
> *And live on abalone.*
>
> *Oh! Mission Point's a friendly joint,*
> *Where every crab's a crony;*
> *And true and kind you'll ever find*
> *The clinging abalone.*
>
> *He wanders free beside the sea*
> *Where'er the coast is stony;*
> *He flaps his wings and madly sings—*
> *The plaintive abalone.*

THE BOHEMIANS

By Carmel Bay, the people say
We feed the lazzaroni
On Boston beans and fresh sardines
And toothsome abalone.

Some live on hope, some live on dope,
And some on alimony;
But my tom-cat, he lives on fat
And tender abalone.

Oh! Some drink rain, and some champagne,
Or brandy by the pony;
But I will try a little rye
With a dash of abalone.

Oh! Some like jam, and some like ham,
And some like macaroni;
But bring to me a pail of gin
And a tub of abalone.

He hides in caves beneath the waves,
His ancient patrimony;
And so 'tis shown that faith alone
Reveals the abalone.

The more we take, the more they make
In deep sea matrimony;
Race suicide cannot betide
The fertile abalone.

I telegraph my better half
By Morse or by Marconi;
But if the need arise for speed,
I send an Abalone.

Oh, some folks think the Lord is fat,
Some think that He is bony;
But as for me, I think that He
Is like an abalone.

Guest book from the Café Ernest, August 28, 1913. Here California poet George Sterling wrote the most famous stanza of the abalone song. *Pat Sands Collection.*

Besides Sterling and Opal Heron, some of the other writers included Ambrose Bierce, Gelett Burgess, Mary Austin and Sinclair Lewis. And it wasn't just abalone to which George Sterling was writing poetry. He was also wooing Pop's young daughter Mimi, who in 1913 was just sixteen years old when Sterling wrote this poem for her, being published here for the very first time.

To Mimi

O Beauty Dear and Brief!
So beautiful you are
I think of lilies and their fragrant souls,
Of foam and sunset where the ocean rolls,
Of morning and of evening star:
You borrow from the loveliness of each
Leaving me poor of speech.
Fairer you are than those—
More fair than any flower the twilights view.
Surely such eyes as yours have wept the dew
Hid in the bosom of the rose.
And your young mouth seems sharpen not for grief,
O beauty dear and brief!
You cannot know your heart,
And that wild music youth's Adventure brings
Shall close within your breast its unseen wings.
How soon the youth and strains depart!
How soon the arms of Silence clasp the tune,
And loveliness, how soon!

George Sterling was a noted "ladies' man." He probably gave this poem to many girls.

The Café Ernest always attracted the art community in Monterey, and Pop always had a soft spot for artists. In an oral history conducted in 1968 with Elise Whitaker Martinez, wife of California artist Xavier Martinez, she said this of Pop: "Dear old Pop Ernest, a figure in Monterey, loved the artists. He would fix the most wonderful meals for us and Marty's [Xavier Martinez] class for next to nothing because we were artists and he was looking after us. He would cook up the most wonderful fish dinners one can imagine, beautifully done and decorated for his bunch of artists."

In 1912, the anti-Japanese sentiment in California and Monterey reached new heights. On November 7 of that year, a meeting was held to discuss changing the laws of the fishing practices being used on the Monterey Bay. The headline in the *Monterey Daily Cypress* that day was, "Fish Laws Are Bad, Changes Will Benefit Monterey." Some of the laws they wanted to change included one that noted that it was "unlawful to catch, sell or handle abalones not to be used for canning purposes or to be sold fresh in the shells." Another prohibited "the taking of abalones in Monterey county for commercial purposes for a period of three years."

The *Cypress* went on to note, "For the past few years the Japanese have been taking immense quantities of abalones and drying them and shipping them to Japan and at the present time it is almost impossible to get any abalones along the coast of the Monterey Peninsula. It is proposed to stop this."

Sometime in early winter of 1913, a man named H.L. Hirsch, the manager of the Hof Brau Restaurant and Café in San Francisco, had an abalone steak dinner at the Café Ernest while visiting Monterey. He was so taken with his dinner that he immediately offered Doelter a job that would pay him a great deal of money, more than he made in a year running his own restaurant and tavern, to bring his abalone recipes to San Francisco. The offer was too good for Ernest to turn down. Right after the new year of 1914, Pop packed up his family and his abalone recipes and moved back to San Francisco.

THE HOF BRAU

By 1914, San Francisco had risen from the ashes of the 1906 earthquake and fire to become a cosmopolitan city with many different restaurants that could accommodate everyone's tastes. The Doelter family, having already lived in San Francisco, felt very comfortable there. Carl and Ernest Jr. both got jobs at the St. Francis Hotel, Carl as busboy and Ernest Jr. working in the kitchen. Although Ernest was offered this new job, he wasn't able to start at the Hof Brau right away because of the abalone season. In 1914, the California abalone season went from July 1 to March 1, and the Hof Brau, even though there were still a few months left in the season, wanted to introduce its new chef and newest food sensation at the beginning of the 1914 season.

Instead, Ernest took a temporary job as a waiter at one of San Francisco's oldest restaurants, the Poodle Dog. The original Poodle Dog

Postcard for the Hof Brau. The restaurant was in the basement of the Pacific Building in San Francisco and had several special rooms. Circa 1914. *Author's collection.*

was a six-story brick building with accommodations for every taste, including a private elevator hidden in the rear of the building that would take couples to secluded suites, each equipped with its own bedroom with a canopied brass bed and a private bathroom. This Poodle Dog was destroyed by the San Francisco earthquake and fire. By the time Ernest arrived at the Poodle Dog, it had been rebuilt and moved to Bush Street. This is how one journalist at that time described it: "One of the interesting features of the Poodle Dog was the daily gathering there at noon of many of the city's foremost men, who sat around an immense table and discussed affairs of a social and business nature. The destiny of many important business undertakings was settled at these noon dinners." Ernest was only there for a few months, but this idea of a businessman lunch gathering stuck with him.

The Hof Brau was a German restaurant that catered mainly to the tourist trade. Located at the corner of Fourth and Market Streets in the basement of the Pacific Building, it was a large restaurant that had banquet rooms and special dining rooms for ladies and families and held concerts everyday with the "Famous Hof Brau Orchestra."

On July 16, 1914, this ad appeared in the *San Francisco Chronicle*:

A NEW DELICIOUS SEAFOOD

*Pop Ernest, recently of Monterey, formerly of the Pacific Yacht Club, is
the discoverer of a way of preparing Abalones that makes of this seafood
a feast for epicures. We have secured the exclusive services of this one and
only Abalone Chef.
This new food will hereafter be served in regular dinners and a la
carte, in numerous styles—including "Abalone Nectar" and several other
delicious soups.
We shall cater to indoor mussel bakes and Abalone Feasts. Our patrons
are promised a new treat, a new gustatory sensation.*

*Moderate Prices
A New Delicious Seafood. Fine Music
NO CABARET
Fourth and Market*

This is the first time he was introduced officially as "Pop" Ernest. World War I
was developing in Europe, and the beginnings of anti-German sentiment were
building in the United States. By dropping his surname and calling himself
"Pop," he was creating a persona, a character. "Pop" was a nickname that was
used mostly by his family. But I also think that he was trying to capitalize a bit
on the use of that name. At the turn of the last century, there were two well-
known San Francisco chefs/restaurateurs who went by the nickname "Pop."
One was Pop Floyd, who had recently been killed in an altercation with his
bartender and had a popular restaurant on California Street. The other was
Pop Sullivan, who ran the Pop Sullivan Café in the Grand Hotel and was
particularly popular with San Francisco businessmen.

Doelter had arranged with the Point Lobos Abalone Company to have
the abalone transported by train to San Francisco every day. There was still
a movement in California/Monterey to restrict the Japanese from shipping
abalone out of the state, so this "fresh abalone" was a possible new market
for all the Japanese abalone companies.

Pop developed a special abalone menu for the Hof Brau:

*Abalone Cocktail and Abalone Salad: 25 cents
Abalone Nector in a cup, hot or cold: 25 cents*

The Cleanest Wholesomest Shellfish

is the abalone. Clings to the rocks and feeds on seaweed and mosses. We get them daily by express, direct from Point Lobos, Carmel Bay; packed in seaweed, they arrive here not only fresh, but "alive and kicking."

If you want a new gastronomic sensation visit the

MARKET AND FOURTH STS.
Moderate Prices.   Good Music.
NO CABARET

Ads for the Hof Brau would appear in the *San Francisco Chronicle* at least once a week. Circa 1914.

The Hof Bräu

Oysters
ToKe Points, Half Shell 35
Blue Points, Half Shell 35
Large Eastern, Half Shell 35
Stewed or Fried 40
Fancy or Pepper Roast 25
Eastern CocKtail 25
California Cocktail 25

Relishes
Asparagus Vinaigrette or Mayonnaise 25

Queen or Stuffed Olives. 15
Ehmann's Ripe California Olives. .15
Senfgurken 15
Chow Chow or Chutney 15

Dill Pickles 10
Anchovies on Toast 25
Sardellen on Toast 25
Pickled Walnuts 15

Salads
CRAB 25
SHRIMP 35
LETTUCE 15
LETTUCE AND TOMATO.....25
Lettuce (with egg or mayonnaise) 20

HEARTS OF LETTUCE 20
TOMATO (with Green Peppers) .20
TOMATO (with Mayonnaise) ...20
SLICED TOMATO 15

COMBINATION 25
COMBINATION HOF-BRAU .35
ASPARAGUS 30
HERRING 25

THURSDAY, AUGUST 13, 1914.

READY TODAY FOR IMMEDIATE SERVICE

Soups LENTILS & FRANKFURTERS 15;   CREAM OF TOMATO   15
CONSOMME, CLEAR 15; CLAM CHOWDER 25; CLAM BROTH   25.

Fish
BROILED ENGLISH SOLE A'l'MAITRE d'HOTEL   40
Striped Bass 40;   FRIED WHITE BAIT 40;   Boned Smelts   35
BLACK ROCK BASS FRIED IN BUTTER 40;   SALMON STEAK   40
Filet of Sole, Tartar Sauce 35;   Sand Dabs, Meuniere   35
STEAMED FINNAN HADDIE, PARSLEY BUTTER SAUCE   40
Clams or Mussels, Plain or Bordelaise   35

Entrees
NEW HOLLAND HERRING, BOILED POTATO   30
Tomato Stuffed with Celery, Mayonnaise   20
SHAD ROE WITH BACON & ASPARAGUS   50
Deviled Crab in Shell 40; SCHMIEREKAESE (Cottage Cheese) 15
FRIED PISMO BEACH CLAMS, TOMATO SAUCE   40
Potted Breast of Lamb, Navy Beans   40
CORNED BEEF & CABBAGE 40;   NEW ENGLAND BOILED DINNER 45
Cold Pickled Pigs Feet 30;   STUFFED BELL PEPPERS (2) 20
FRESH SHRIMP OR LOBSTER SALAD, MAYONNAISE   35
German Pot Roast, Noodles   40
BAKED PORK & BEANS, BOSTON BROWN BREAD   30
Calf's Brains au Beurre Noir   35
RACK OF LAMB, CASSEROLE   50
Baked Short Ribs of Beef, Schnitt Bohnen   40
POACHED EGGS BENEDICT   40
Kalbs Haxen, Hungarian Style   45
OYSTER PATTIES A LA BECHAMEL   (To Order)   50

Roast Half Lobster, Mayonnaise   60
HOF-BRAU SPECIAL BAKED POTATO   (To Order)   10

LEG OF PORK, DRESSING & STEWED PRUNES   40
Prime Beef au Jus 40;   Extra Cut   75
HALF PAPRICA CHICKEN, HUNGARIAN STYLE   (To Order)   75
Half Spring Chicken, Fried or Broiled   "   60

Vegetables
French Peas ....20 Sugar Corn ....10 Sauerkraut 10
Green Peas ....10 String Beans ....10 Asparagus 25

FRESH GREEN CORN ON COB 20;   CAULIFLOWER IN CREAM   15
Lyonnaise, German, French or Straw Fried Potatoes   10
FRIED EGG PLANT 15; CORN SAUTE 20;   SUMMER SQUASH   10
Fried Sweet Potatoes   15;   Southern Style   25

Dessert
Macaroon Torte ....15 French Pastry (1), 10; (2)...15 Ice Cream, Vanilla, Strawberry
Hof-Bräu Torte ....15 Baked Apple and Cream ....15 or Chocolate, with Cake....15

FARINA PUDDING, FRESH STRAWBERRY SAUCE 15; WATERMELON   15

ABALONE SPECIALS

ABALONE COCKTAIL 25;   ABALONE SALAD   25

SOUPS

ABALONE NECTAR IN CUP, HOT OR COLD   25
CREAM OF ABALONE   25
ABALONE CHOWDER   25

FILET OF ABALONE A LA ERNEST   50
ABALONE SPANISH   50
ABALONE A LA NEWBURG   75
ABALONE A l'AMERICAINE   75

(vertical text, left margin) Underberg-Boonekamp   Per Pony 15 cents   An Appetizer and Digestive

(vertical text, right margin) For Wine List or Articles not on this Menu ask for General Bill of Fare

Hof Brau menu.
Circa 1914.
*California Historical
Society Collection.*

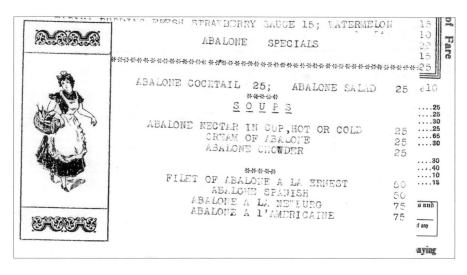

Hof Brau menu, with abalone specials glued onto the page. This is the first time abalone appeared on a menu like this. Circa 1914. *California Historical Society Collection.*

Cream of Abalone: 25 cents
Abalone Chowder: 25 cents
Filet of Abalone A La Ernest: 50 Cents
Abalone Spanish: 50 cents
Abalone A La Newberg: 75 cents
Abalone A l'Americaine: 75 cents

This new menu was printed and then glued to the bottom half of the already existing Hof Brau menu. Since the Café Ernest in Monterey never had a printed menu, this is the first time that abalone appeared on one.

In Clarence E. Edwords's 1914 book *Bohemian San Francisco: It's Restaurants and Their Most Famous Recipes: The Elegant Art of Dining*, he wrote this about the Hof Brau:

> *The Hof Brau, however, is less distinctively German as the greater number of its patrons are Americans. The specialty of the Hof Brau is abalones, and they have as a feature this shell fish cooked in several ways. They also have as the chef in charge of the abalone dishes, Herbert [Ernest], formerly chef for one of the yacht clubs of the coast, who claims to have the only proper recipe for making abalones tender. Under ordinary circumstances the abalone is tough and unpalatable, but after the deft manipulation of*

Herbert they are tender and make a fine dish, either fried, as chowder or a la Newberg.

In a later chapter, he went on to write this about abalone:

Abalones are a univalve that has been much in vogue among the Chinese but has seldom found place on the tables of restaurants owing to the difficulty in preparing them, as they are tough and insipid under ordinary circumstances. When made tender either by the Chinese method of pounding, or by steeping in vinegar, they serve the purpose of clams but have not the fine flavor. The Hof Brau restaurant is now making a specialty of abalones, but it takes sentiment to say that one really finds anything extra good in them.

Another possible motivating factor in Pop's decision to take the job at the Hof Brau was the long-planned Panama Pacific International Exposition that was to open in San Francisco in early 1915.

Chapter 8

The Panama Pacific
International Exposition

The Panama Canal opened with much fanfare on October 13, 1913, and connected the Atlantic with the Pacific. But years before the canal was even open, there were plans to hold a large exposition, a world's fair, in the United States to honor its opening. Many cities vied to host this exposition, including San Francisco. It would be a huge economic boost for a city that was still rebuilding itself after the 1906 earthquake and fire.

In 1910, a group of San Francisco businessmen and civic leaders met to discuss the possibility of hosting this exposition. In just two short hours, these men were able to raise close to $4 million to show their commitment to this world's fair. But there was a lot of competition from other cities, especially New Orleans. The City of San Francisco and the State of California worked furiously to make this fair happen. There were all kinds of campaigns and advertising geared toward the United States Congress, whose members were the ultimate decision-makers, to award San Francisco this grand exposition. Evidently, the campaign worked because in 1911, President William Howard Taft announced that San Francisco would be the host city of the Panama Pacific International Exposition.

It took close to three years and almost $50 million to build this fair. Built on 635 acres of filled-in mudflats on what is now the Marina District of San Francisco, the fair featured eleven different exhibition halls, called "Palaces," including the Palace of Fine Arts, the Palace of Education, the Palace of Social Economy, the Palace of Liberal Arts, the Palace of Manufactures and Varied Industries, the Palace of Machinery, the Palace of Transportation, the

Postcard for the Panama Pacific International Exhibition. There were many variations and styles to promote the exhibition. Circa 1914. *Author's collection.*

Palace of Agriculture, the Palace of Live Stock, the Palace of Horticulture and the Palace of Mines and Metallurgy.

There was also the Tower of Jewels, which was the main building at the Panama Pacific International Exposition and stood 435 feet tall. It was covered with more than 100,000 cut-glass "jewels" called "Novagems" that glittered in the sunlight; it was also illuminated at night by more than fifty spotlights.

The Fun Zone was a sixty-five-acre amusement park area that cost $12 million to build and was filled with rides, games and concessions. There was a submarine ride, exotic dancers and musicians. You could ride a train through large-scale models of Yellowstone Park and the Grand Canyon, and there was a five-acre working replica of the Panama Canal. At the Cawston Ostrich Farm exhibit, you could ride on the back of a live ostrich. The Aeroscope was probably the most exciting feature for the majority of attendees. It was like a large house on a mechanical arm that weighed seven hundred tons and could take close to 120 passengers 330 feet above the exposition grounds, giving everyone incredible views of San Francisco. Its designer and builder was Joseph B. Strauss, the same man who went on to design the Golden Gate Bridge.

Some of the other exhibits at the exposition included a telephone line that was set up between New York City and San Francisco so people in New York could hear the Pacific Ocean. You could type a letter on a giant Underwood typewriter, and after an extensive letter campaign from local school kids, the Liberty Bell was transported by train on a nationwide tour to be part of the exposition. The Ford Motor Company built cars on an assembly line every ten minutes. The exposition was a big event. Even though we were in the early stages of World War I, many countries were represented, each with iconic buildings and foods. All these buildings were built of wood, plaster and burlap so they could be easily torn down.

Although the Hof Brau was a popular restaurant with both locals and tourists, people were still bit apprehensive about eating the abalone. The Hof Brau, though, was fully committed. It ran weekly ads in the *San Francisco Chronicle* to promote its abalone dishes, such as the following:

The Cleanest Wholesomest Shellfish Is the Abalone

Clings to the rocks and feeds on seaweed and mosses. We get them daily by direct express, direct from Point Lobos, Carmel Bay. Packed in seaweed, they arrive here not only fresh, but alive and kicking. If you want a new gastronomic sensation visit the Hof Brau.

Market and Fourth Sts
Moderate Prices. Good Music
No Cabaret

The Panama Pacific International Exposition opened on February 20, 1915, and the whole world descended on San Francisco. Special trains and ships from the East Coast were scheduled to bring people to the fair. The State of California had the largest of the state buildings, five acres in size. Every county was represented—each county sent special businesses as representatives. One of the businesses that Monterey County sent was A.M. Allan and Gennosuke Kodani's Point Lobos Monterey Abalone Company. Their booth at the exposition featured canned abalone that they gave away as souvenirs. They also sent folks down to the Hof Brau for fresh abalone steak dinners.

Also in 1915, the State of California banned the Japanese from exporting dried abalone out of California. As the popularity of abalone as food grew, in big part because of Pop Ernest, more and more people were taking it

Booth for the Point Lobos Abalone Company at the Panama Pacific International Exhibition. The booth was located in the California State Building. Circa 1915. *Kodani Family Collection.*

from the intertidal zones, and soon all the abalone was gone from the rocks. It was the thinking of most people at that time that abalone migrated from deep water to shallow water, even though marine biologists were saying that this was not the case. It was believed that the Japanese divers were taking all the abalone from the deep waters before they could migrate to those shallow waters. In fact, some of these scientists were saying the exact opposite—it was the tourists and local folks taking all the abalone from the rocks along the intertidal that was causing the disappearance. There was no chance of the abalone becoming extinct in the deep waters of the Monterey Bay.

Pop Ernest's invention of the fresh abalone steak could become the savior of the California Japanese abalone industry. It is estimated that 2 million people came to San Francisco to visit the fair. Many of them had dinner at the Hof Brau. Soon everyone wanted fresh abalone steaks. Hotels and restaurants all wanted this new food sensation. The demand was so great that the Hof Brau couldn't get it fast enough. Because abalone was being shipped by train from Monterey, the shipments were often late due to delayed trains and bad weather, leaving customers disappointed and unhappy. When the abalone season ended on March 1, 1915, the Hof Brau needed to find a replacement. Pop came to the rescue. On April 14, 1915, this ad appeared in the *San Francisco Chronicle*:

> *THESE BIG LUSCIOUS MONTEREY MUSSELS!*
>
> *Abalones are out of season but Pop Ernest is still with us, and his next big specialty that food savants talk about is Spiced Mussel Salad*
>
> *"A gustatory dream"*
>
> *The same big meaty mussels are served also Bordelaise in butter sauce and plan steamed.*

The mussels were also coming from the Point Lobos Abalone Company. The restaurant continued to get the canned abalone, so Pop (and the Hof Brau) could still offer abalone chowder and salads, but it was the fresh steak that everybody really wanted. The State of California agreed to open the abalone season one month earlier, in June 1915, probably in part because of the demand for the fresh product. And just like that, the Hof Brau and Pop were again serving fresh abalone steaks to the world.

The Panama Pacific International Exposition closed on December 4, 1915. It was a huge success for everyone involved, the City of San Francisco and especially the Hof Brau and Pop Ernest. All kinds of new products and services were introduced at the exposition besides the abalone steak. The Monterey sardine was also introduced to the world there, and within a few short years, it would eventually become the largest fishing industry of a single fish in the history of the United States.

A NEW RESTAURANT

Pop was tired of working for someone else. He wanted to be his own boss, and it was time to move on—at least from the Hof Brau. He initially struck a deal to open a restaurant in the Hotel Fielding at Geary and Mason Street, but the rent proved too high, and with the added cost of hiring new help,

Pop Ernest's

372 Bush Street — Between Kearny and Montgomery

A place to eat—morning, noon and night. Specializes on sea food, game and poultry. Big deep sea mussels as not known before in San Francisco. Exclusive: Abalone a 'la Ernest in various solid and liquid forms. Pop is recognized as the discoverer of Abalone as a white man's delicacy.

Business Lunch 11-2, 35 Cents

Business card for Pop Ernest's. This is the first time that he was officially noted as "Pop" Ernest. Circa 1916. *Pat Sands Collection.*

he felt that it would be unprofitable. But this was also a time for joy, as his youngest daughter, Minnie, got married to man named Fred McMurray, a musician from Monterey who had been Carl Doelter's violin teacher.

Pop finally found a new place where the rent was much cheaper at 372 Bush Street, and in the spring of 1916, he opened "Pop Ernest's Restaurant." And just like in Monterey, all three of his sons worked in the restaurant. Ernest Jr. and Otto worked as the cooks, while Carl, alongside Pop, worked as a waiter. Pop was also the host, always out front greeting the customers, as it was something he couldn't do at the Hof Brau. As Pop was a master at marketing himself and his restaurants, it was around this time that he began to really hone this persona of "Pop Ernest." Pop was already a large man with a bushy mustache and goatee, and he always wore a white apron with a white chef's jacket, but then he added to his regalia a red fez—the cherry on top. No one knows why he wore the fez, not even his family. It was, in part, a marketing tool, but I also think that he liked to wear it. People remembered him. More importantly, people remembered his restaurant. He probably got the idea of the fez from the Panama Pacific International Exposition. Many of the actual builders of the exposition belonged to an organization that was an offshoot of the Masons called Sciots. According to historian Mickey Downey:

> *In 1905, Charles H.S. Pratt founded an organization within the Masonic fraternity that he called Boosters. Their motto was, and is, "Boost One Another" and they were dedicated to helping out their fellow Masons*

however possible. One year later, the earthquake struck and this organization was instrumental in coordinating hundreds of men that were now out of work and getting them to the locations where work needed to be done to get the city back in operation. This sub-set of the greater fraternity changed their name in 1910 to Sciots, based loosely on Egyptian culture/mythology and adopted the wearing of fezzes. Also, regardless of the tendency for the Masonic fraternity to be known as an insider circle for business, this group is the only one that expressly sought to support the businesses of its members, as well as volunteer support, and charity.

If you were going to survive in business in California, you had to be a Mason, then an all-white, all-male organization. There is no evidence that Pop was ever a Mason or a member of the Sciots, but he would have sought out their support, even to the point of wearing a red fez. It eventually became a part of him—almost an extension of who he was. He was synonymous with the fez and abalone.

Pop Ernest's advertised his new restaurant as "A place to eat—morning, noon and night. Specializes in sea food, game and poultry. Big deep sea mussels as not known before in San Francisco. Exclusive: Abalone à la Ernest in various solid and liquid forms. Pop is recognized as the discoverer of Abalone as a white man's delicacy." The "Abalone a 'la Ernest" was printed in red. His reputation from the Hof Brau and abalone followed him to Bush Street, and business was good. He really wanted to create a businessman's restaurant, like the Poodle Dog, but

A wonderful portrait of Pop on the front deck of the restaurant holding an abalone shell. Note the sake barrel on Pop's right. He used these barrels throughout the restaurant as planters. *Pat Sands Collection.*

again he had shipment problems and couldn't always get the fresh abalone he needed. Because it was the abalone that was bringing in the customers, business began to slip. With World War I raging in Europe, the anti-German sentiment in United States was growing stronger and stronger. Pop saw the writing on the wall, and after a year on Bush Street, he closed his restaurant. The Hof Brau eventually changed its name to the States Restaurant and took on an American theme.

At first, Pop wasn't sure what to do. His family was separated. Daughter Vera and her now husband, Walter Stokes, moved to Oakland, where Walter worked in the shipyards. Ernest Jr. and Otto had both joined the Merchant Marines, and Carl had moved to Eureka to work as a waiter in the Hotel Vance.

Luckily, there was still a great demand for fresh abalone. Pop made a trip to Point Lobos and struck a deal with A.M. Allan and Gennosuke Kodani to work as an abalone broker, preparing fresh abalone steaks and selling them to hotels and restaurant all over California. This idea worked for both Point Lobos and Pop. Point Lobos still couldn't ship the dried abalone out of the country, and Pop wanted to continue his fresh abalone business, so it was the perfect symbiotic relationship. This was his chance to bring Pop Ernest–style abalone to the masses. They needed each other to survive.

BACK TO MONTEREY

Because he was working directly with the Point Lobos abalone operation, he moved into a small house on the property. His wife, Veronica, initially stayed in San Francisco to work as a go-between/salesperson, talking directly to the hotels and restaurants. Living at Point Lobos in 1917 was a lot like living in a small Japanese village. It was probably a bit uncomfortable for Pop because of his earlier experience with the Japanese waiter at the Pacific Yacht Club; he never quite got over his reluctance to working with the Japanese.

Although it's not exactly clear what his business relationship was with Allan and Kodani, Pop was directly overseeing the fresh abalone business for

Opposite, top: The cabin at Point Lobos. Circa 1917. *Pat Sands Collection.*

Opposite, bottom: Removing the abalone from the shell. Circa 1938. *City of Monterey, California History Room.*

Slicing the abalone steak on the Monterey Wharf. Circa 1938. *City of Monterey, California History Room.*

the Point Lobos Abalone Company. He developed a kind of assembly line of preparing fresh abalone for shipment. Once the abalone came into the cannery, it was removed from the shell, sliced into steaks with a commercial meat slicer and then pounded with wooden mallets on special "pounding tables." The tables were designed just for pounding abalone. An individual would sit on a bench that was connected with wooden slats or rails to a three-foot-high by one-foot-wide solid wooden beam. After pounding, the abalone steaks would be placed into wooden crates ready for shipment to the restaurants and hotels in San Francisco and Los Angeles. Pop also worked on his abalone recipes.

Vera didn't stay in San Francisco long. She, daughter Vera and Vera's new baby, Lois, moved to Point Lobos to help with the abalone operation. When the United States entered World War I in 1917, Carl was drafted and sent to France with the Ninety-first Infantry Division, where he fought in the Battle of the Argonne Forest, the longest and bloodiest battle in United States military history.

Being an abalone diver can be very hard. All that water pressure will eventually take its toll on the human body. An abalone diver's diving life is usually about ten years. Since the 1907 "Gentlemen's Agreement" between

Japanese ladies pounding abalone on the Monterey Wharf. Circa 1938. *City of Monterey, California History Room.*

the United States and Japan, divers (and other male workers) who had not already immigrated to the United States were not being issued passports. By 1919, thanks to Pop's recipe, the demand for fresh abalone steaks had become insatiable. Other abalone companies in California and Monterey were now pounding fresh abalone for their customers. There was a need for new divers. In the Santa Barbara area of California, U.S.-born white divers were suiting up and diving for abalone. According to Japanese historian Toshio Oba, a number of divers entered the United States illegally either as stowaways from Japan or through Mexico or Canada. Because the California abalone industry was so unique, the Point Lobos Abalone Company was able to strike a deal with the United States government allowing them to bring in new divers as "guest workers" from Japan on the condition that these divers would return to Japan after an allotted amount time. To guarantee that they would return, Point Lobos put up a bond for each diver.

At home in Japan, many of the women of Chikura, where a number of divers came from, formed an association called "America-gomori" or

"America-Ko." While their fathers, husbands and sons were far away in California/Monterey, they would meet regularly on the eighth day of every month, the anniversary day of the Takamimusuhi shrine. They prayed that their family members would return home in good health.

In 1919, Pop once again packed up his family and his abalone recipes and moved from Point Lobos. This time, it was not so far—just a few miles to Monterey. He wanted to open a new restaurant on the Monterey Wharf. This would become the first restaurant on the wharf. The Monterey Yacht Club, which was built at the foot of the Monterey Wharf, was available.

The first Monterey Wharf was built in 1845 by Thomas Larkin, a Monterey merchant who was tired of losing his cargo into the Monterey Harbor when it was being transferred from the ship to the longboat that would bring it ashore. So, he built a crude cribwork and rock wharf. In the 1870s, the Pacific Steamship Company built a more traditional wooden wharf so passengers and cargo could easily disembark. When the Hotel Del Monte opened in 1880, it built a wooden walkway/sidewalk that went from the hotel along the waterfront to the Monterey Wharf, creating a more tourist-oriented wharf. There were fish markets, deep-sea fishing excursions, small sailboat rentals and glass-bottom boat rides. The yacht club was built at the foot of the Monterey Wharf on property that was part of the custom house and therefore owned by the U.S. government in 1910. It was built by F.E. Booth, who had a salmon/sardine cannery right next to the wharf. There weren't a lot of big yachts in Monterey at that time, but there were a lot of sailboats, and the owners of these boats enjoyed having their own club. Boats could be rented for fishing and pleasure use.

Before 1915, salmon was the big fishing industry in Monterey and California; sardines formed a small secondary fishing industry, procured in the fall and winter months. But salmon was king, the big money fish, and it was Japanese fishermen who were doing it. At the end of the 1909 salmon season (and the season then lasted three months, from May 15 to August 15), the *Monterey Daily Cypress* reported that there were 185 salmon boats fishing the Monterey Bay; 145 were Japanese owned. That 1909 salmon season caught 1.5 million pounds of king salmon!

Booth was also experimenting with these large sardine that were appearing in the bay at the end of the end of the salmon season, and he needed sardine fishermen because most of the Japanese salmon fishermen were leaving Monterey at the end of the salmon season to work in the agricultural fields in central California. In 1905, Booth said to the *Monterey New Era*, "I'm not going to hire anymore Japanese." Easy call for him because he

Business card for Pop's new restaurant, The Club. Just a few months later, the name was changed to Pop Ernest's. Circa 1919. *Pat Sands Collection.*

The front of The Club. Pop is on the left, and Carl is on the right. Note the boat in front filled with flowers. Circa 1919. *Pat Sands Collection.*

didn't really mean it. He was still going to buy salmon from those Japanese fishermen when they returned in the spring. It was then that he sent for some Sicilian fishermen, who had already worked for him fishing salmon along the Sacramento River, to come to Monterey and fish sardine. Most of that salmon was going to Europe, mainly to Germany. Most of the sardines that were being eaten in the United States then were coming from Europe, mainly from France, which was the big sardine producer at the turn of the last century. When war broke out in Europe in 1914, it cut off all that salmon going to Europe and all those sardines coming from Europe, and they just switched and began to heavily fish sardine along the West Coast. There were sardine canneries in New York State and Maine, but they couldn't fish because there were German submarines out in the Atlantic.

As the sardine fishery grew and began to dominate the Monterey Bay, the wharf began to change, going from a gentle tourist-oriented wharf to a busy commercial wharf now owned by the City of Monterey, which took over the wharf and its buildings after a dispute with the Pacific Steamship Company in 1916. The need for a yacht club dissipated, and the building became neglected. By the time Pop leased the building from the city, the United States government actually owned the land the building sat on. It was in desperate need of repairs. Pop first approached T.A. Work, the man who leased him his first restaurant in Monterey in 1907, for a loan to make the necessary repairs on the building. T.A. was a businessman; although he liked and believed in Pop, he turned him down. He asked him, "Who's going to go down to that dirty old waterfront and eat?" Somehow Pop got the money he needed, and with the war over in Europe, all the boys had come home. Carl Doelter later described the building: "It was just a big empty shell of a building when we bought it, with large cracks in the floor of the kitchen where waves would splash in at high tide, but the upstairs portion where we would be seating most of our customers, was solidly built of Monterey Cypress. We all went to work cleaning up, Pop, Ernest Jr., Otto, Walter Stokes and I. The whole place had to be rewired and new plumbing installed. Even the door knobs had to be replaced, not to mention adding a hardwood floor in the dining room."

Pop opened his new wharf restaurant on Saturday, May 31, 1919. But just two days before, on May 29, this announcement appeared in the *Monterey Daily Cypress and American*:

"Abalone King"
To Open "The Club"
Saturday Night

"Pop" Ernest, who holds undisputed title as "The Abalone King," has announced that Saturday is to be the big opening night at The Club, which is the name of his new fish restaurant. A delicious dinner will be served, making a specialty of sea foods. Reservations are being made and tables are going fast. As no wines will be provided on the opening night patrons are informed that they may bring such as they like with them. There is to be music and dancing and a number of surprise features will add to the enjoyment of the patrons. A huge fireplace at one end of the dining room which is on the second floor, will add to the coziness and comfort of the guests.

Interior of the restaurant. Note the nautical theme with the sea stars hanging in the window. Many Monterey artists would exchange paintings of Pop or Monterey scenes that would then be hung on the walls of the restaurant. Circa 1925. *Pat Sands Collection.*

Notably, this is the first time, at least publicly, that he was crowned the "Abalone King." It's unknown whether this title came from the newspaper writer or from Pop himself, but it's a crown he wore for the rest of his life.

He initially named it The Club because it was in the old Monterey Yacht Club, and most people still referred to the building as the Club. Also, the name "Club" was already painted in large letters on the roof where everyone could see it.

That name didn't last long, though, and in just a few short months, he changed the name to Pop Ernest's Sea Food Restaurant. The new place could seat up to two hundred people and was built on stilts over a large rock formation in the Monterey Harbor. It had a large open porch where people could eat and look out onto the Monterey Bay. It was always very festive, with strings of Japanese lanterns hanging throughout. The interior of the restaurant had a nautical theme, with whalebone ribs draping the fireplace, abalone shells, fishnets and lights sconces made

ABALONE
a sea food
fresh from the rocks of
Carmel Bay tender
and satisfying

The
States
Restaurant

Market at Fourth
San Francisco

GOOD MUSIC
NO CABARET

This ad for the States Restaurant (formerly the Hof Brau) appeared in the *Monterey Daily Cypress* just days after Pop opened The Club. *Author's collection.*

of seashells. The restaurant actually had two rooms for serving—one on the lower level that catered to the working class and one on the upper level that catered to the Hotel Del Monte clientele. T.A. Work was his very first customer.

Just a few days after he opened The Club, the States Restaurant, formerly the Hof Brau of San Francisco, ran a series of ads in the *Monterey Daily Cypress* promoting its abalone dinners, one of which stated:

> *Abalone*
> *a sea food*
> *fresh from the rocks of*
> *Carmel Bay tender*
> *and satisfying*

The States Restaurant was where Pop made abalone famous, and it was making a statement. Not only was it still serving abalone, but it was also buying it from the Point Lobos Abalone Company. At that time, it was not that unusual for people from Monterey to travel via the Del Monte Express to spend a day or two in San Francisco. In part, the States was riding Pop's coattails.

Chapter 9

"Ernest" or "Ernst"?

There has always been a big debate around Monterey: How do you pronounce Pop's name? About ten years ago, I was giving a lecture about abalone to a small service club, and when I talked about Pop, I called him "Ernest." An elderly woman in the audience who had lived in Monterey for several years kept correcting me, saying, "It's *Ernst*!" After my lecture, I asked the women what she remembered about the restaurant, besides the abalone. She said that everyone called it "Pop" Ernst's. When I pointed out to her that the spelling is "Ernest," that didn't seem to matter.

When Pop received his naturalization papers on January 26, 1887, he (or the clerk who issued the papers) added the extra *e* to Americanize his name. From then on, he was Ernest. When he married his beloved wife, Veronica, in 1890, he spelled his name as "Ernest" on the marriage license. His first restaurant in Monterey was Café Ernest. When he was introduced to the world in San Francisco in 1914, he was Pop Ernest. On census and business records of that time, it's always "Ernest." And when he came back to Monterey and opened his wharf restaurant, it was "Pop" Ernest, and even the family today refers to him as Ernest. But I think the answer is both. People still called him Ernst, and on occasion, reporters writing stories about the restaurant and abalone would often print his name as "Ernst." On some occasions, both "Ernst" and "Ernest" would appear in the same article. So, in spite of adding the extra *e* to his name, and probably because he was German, to some he will always be Ernst.

The restaurant was a big success, and people came from all over Northern California to eat abalone and visit with Pop. Besides greeting guests, he,

Pop with two large red abalone shells on the deck of the restaurant. Circa 1930. *Pat Sands Collection.*

Pop's abalone boat the *Pop Ernest*. He also used this boat for basking shark hunts. *Pat Sands Collection.*

Ernest Jr. and Otto worked the kitchen, Carl as the headwaiter and Mother Veronica as hostess. The big business was in the summer, and extra help would be hired only to be let go in September. When he opened his new restaurant on the Monterey Wharf, he also bought a boat that he named the *Pop Ernest* and hired his own dive crew to get abalone—not only for the restaurant but also to continue broking abalone steaks to restaurants and hotels throughout California. He began working with a Santa Cruz seafood distributer called S. Berk & Company. It had offices in San Francisco and advertised Abalone Specialties by Pop Ernest, "the Noted Expert." It wasn't just abalone steaks that it was selling, but "Pop" Ernest–style steaks. He was delivering his product to S. Berk ready to go, pounded and seasoned. By hiring his own dive crew and working with S. Berk & Company, he had completely separated himself from the Point Lobos Abalone Company.

Business card for S. Berk & Company. Note that Pop is listed as the "noted expert" when it comes to abalone. Circa 1920. *Pat Sands Collection.*

Salvage diver Eddie Bushnell, one of Pop's abalone divers. *Bushnell Family Collection.*

The diver Pop hired was a man named Eddie Bushnell, who was not Japanese, and was the first (if not the only) non-Japanese abalone diver in the Monterey Bay area. Eddie was a salvage diver by trade and worked closely with the Monterey fishing industry. He loved diving the Monterey Bay and invented one of the first underwater camera housings. He also was responsible for all the maintenance of the sardine hoppers that were so important to the sardine fishing industry. The hoppers first appeared in Monterey Bay in 1926, when these large sardine boats called "purse seiners" also first appeared. These boats were just too big to get close to the canneries to unload. Knut Hovden, a fisheries expert from Norway and a pioneering Monterey sardine cannery owner, had seen these hoppers in the agriculture fields of California. You put your fruit and vegetables into the hopper, and they went by conveyer belt into the cannery. He figured, "Why can't they work in the Monterey Bay?"

Hovden's engineers designed these systems that worked with a marine pump and steel pipe. The pipe connects the hopper to the cannery. The hopper is anchored about five hundred feet off shore from the cannery. The boats brail their catch into the hopper, and the fish were funneled down an angled lattice siding into an opening at the bottom and then sucked into the cannery. These hoppers could take up to seventy tons per hour, and the force was so strong that they would scale the fish as they went through it. It was Eddie's job to pull these hoppers out of the bay every so many years to clean them of barnacles and other marine debris and then float them back out into the bay. He also laid the steel pipe at the bottom of the bay when they first went in, having to use dynamite to make the trenches for the pipe. Monterey Bay is the only place in the world where this hopper system was used.

Unfortunately for Pop, others had learned his method of pounding abalone. By 1920, there was such a demand for fresh abalone that there were nine Japanese abalone companies working off the Monterey Wharf, shipping their product of pounded abalone all over California.

These companies would leave Monterey and usually go south toward Point Sur and beyond. A larger mother boat pulled a small dive boat behind. Each company would be out diving abalone for up to three days. The diver on the boat would make the most money, but it was also the hardest job. The diver would go into the water at about 9:00 a.m. and drop to about thirty feet (sometimes deeper); at that level, you could stay down all day. He would return to the surface at 12:00 p.m. for lunch and then go back into the water at 1:00 p.m., collecting abalone until 4:00 p.m., when he would again return to the surface for the night.

Above: Abalone boat getting ready to unload at the Monterey Wharf. Note the two dive suits draped over the pole so they can dry. Circa 1938. *City of Monterey, California History Room.*

Right: Monterey Abalone diver Roy Hattori returning to the surface after a three-hour dive. The man standing in the boat in the hat is Roy's brother, James, and the other man, with his foot on the ladder, is Ishio Enokida, one of the "tenders" on the boat. Everyone called him "Ish." Circa 1938. *City of Monterey, California History Room.*

Each diver had his own technique to collect abalone. Some would literally "run" once they hit bottom or "duck-walk" or crawl. There was one diver in Monterey who would slither on his stomach like a snake. The idea is not to disturb the abalone but rather to sneak up on them so you can pick them up before they latch on to the rock. Monterey abalone diver Roy Hattori, who was the only diver born in Monterey (all the other divers came from Japan and, with just a few exceptions, returned to Japan) told this author, "You have to run on the bottom to find abalone. And it's not easy. In the very beginning, you tend to use a lot of energy working against the water. But as you get more and more used to diving and get a little more skillful, you learn to use the currents and you learn to use the surge to give you the necessary impetus to travel a little bit faster and easier."

The diver would put the abalone into his basket. Once the basket was full, he would give a signal that he had a full basket by pulling on his lifeline; each diver had their own set of signals. According to Roy:

> *Depending on the size of the abalone, with good-size abalone you get maybe thirteen, fourteen at the most. If you were in a good spot, you would cram the abalone in. In the first place, if you hit a good spot, you would open up the bottom, re-tie the bottom. The bottom opens on these, see. That's how they get the abalone out. They don't pull 'em out through the top. The bottom is made so that you can open it up as much as you want, as long as the abalone doesn't fall through. And so you open up the bottom, you could get maybe 50 percent more abalone just by opening up the bottom to the maximum, where the abalone wouldn't fall through but you could get in everything that you could. And that way, the people around you wouldn't see how many baskets you were putting up. Depending on the boat, some crews carried three men on top. Some carried four men on top, but most of the time, it was three men on top. One man on the scull, and one man tending with the lifeline and one man helping to pull the abalone baskets on board and to measure and to store the abalone into the hold of the diving tender.*

The Japanese crews were very safety-conscious, rarely losing a diver or crewmen in an accident, with some exceptions. In 1910, five Japanese abalone fishermen, including the diver, drowned in a storm off San Simeon. A large wave capsized the boat, knocking the boat crew into the water. Four drowned, and the diver, a man named Yamamoto, was below the surface collecting abalone at the time the wave hit. Of course, the men manning the pump were thrown into the water, and Yamamoto's air supply soon ran out.

Roy's dive boat. You can see Roy's brother, James, and "Ish," the tender, pulling in the lifeline and helping Roy return to the surface. Mr. Saki is on the sculling oar at the stern. The scull kept the boat in place over the diver without using the motor. The Japanese were very careful. A lot of the white divers died when their propellers cut their air hoses. *City of Monterey, California History Room.*

All the dive boats were equipped with a sculling oar, a large wooden oar at the stern of the dive boat that could be operated by one man—again technology that came from Japan. Roy described them like this:

> *They all had sculls. It's a big sweep, like a big oar. They call it sculling. It kept the boat in place with the diver, without using the motor. The Japanese were very careful. A lot of the Caucasian divers died when their propellers cut their air hoses. It was very easy to do, especially when it became windy. But with a sculling oar like this, they sculled and kept the boat in position. The only thing they couldn't do with this type of sweep, they couldn't reverse. There was no reverse. But they always headed into the wind anyway, always kept the nose into the wind keeping the divers bubbles in front.*

Currents could also be a problem for a diver, pushing the diver and kicking up rocks. One diver once had a rock kick up, hitting him in the helmet and

Abalone boats unloading at the Monterey Wharf. Circa 1938. *City of Monterey, California History Room.*

Opposite: Abalone boat retuning to Monterey from a three-day fishing trip. The boxes on the stern are called "live boxes." They are how the dive companies kept the abalone fresh. The abalone would be piled on top of one another inside these handmade redwood boxes and kept in the water before the boats returned to Monterey. Circa 1938. *City of Monterey, California History Room.*

cracking the glass. He immediately dropped to the bottom and fell flat on his face. He then reached into his abalone basket, pulled out a large abalone and slid it over the glass on his helmet, and the abalone sealed up the crack and stopped the water from rushing in. He then released a valve on the helmet that filled up his suit with air in order to help float him back to the surface while pulling on his lifeline for assistance. He went to the surface, changed the glass and started all over again.

Each boat would come back to Monterey with 150 to 200 dozen large red abalone; the abalone would be kept fresh by placing them in "live boxes"; each box could hold 5 to 7 dozen abalone. The live box is an innovation that came from Japan. The abalone would be placed on top of one another inside these redwood boxes and kept in the water to stay fresh. The abalone would feed on the marine plants that grew on the shell of abalone beneath it.

NEW VENTURES, NEW FOODS, MORE ABALONE

When Prohibition took effect on January 17, 1920, Pop, who always relied on his tavern business, was very unhappy about not being able to serve beer and other alcoholic beverages. He would say that it "was a disaster for American cooking." He had to be creative to keep his customers coming through the door.

Pop was always working on his abalone recipes and trying different things. One element of the abalone was the juice that came out of the shell. Abalone will produce a lot of this juice, and Pop would use it to make soups and chowder. He called it the "abalone nectar." He also believed that it could be a natural remedy for indigestion. He sent samples of his abalone nectar to a medical doctor in New York, who agreed with him. This sparked interest from the federal government and the Fish and Game Commission. In October 1924, the California Department of Health held a conference in Monterey, and one of the highlights of the conference was the "abalone nectar" dinner held at the Highlands Inn just south of Point Lobos. Not long after this dinner, Pop began to produce "Abaloniko," a tonic made from abalone nectar. He advertised it as "Nectar of Abalone, A New Epicurean Sea Food Tonic, Stimulating and Nourishing."

In 1919, a whale fishery opened across the bay from Monterey in Moss Landing called California Sea Products. It was a Norwegian company that used large steam-powered chase boats and harpoon cannons to catch whales, and it was very good at what it did. Getting mostly gray and humpback whales, it was able to utilize the whole whale. Oil from the blubber was sold to soap manufactures, the meat was turned into animal feed and the bone was turned into bone meal. Even the tail was eventually used.

Tsunetaro Oda, a Japanese fisheries specialist from the Wakayama Prefecture, along with his partner K. Niino, opened the Sea Pride Cannery (now part of the Monterey Bay Aquarium) on December 17, 1925. It was the first and only completely Japanese-owned cannery on Cannery Row. Sea Pride Cannery, like all the other canneries, canned sardines mostly, but it also canned salmon and abalone. The cannery also specialized in its reduction products.

The waiters. Carl Doelter is standing in front on the right. Circa 1935. *Pat Sands Collection.*

Reduction is a process whereby heads, tails and offal are ground up and baked into a powder, which is then used for fertilizers and animal feeds.

California Sea Products closed in 1926. The last year in operation, it was sending the tail of the whale to Sea Pride in Monterey, where it was canned, probably being marketed to the Japanese communities in California and Japan. But some of that canned whale meat made its way into Pop's kitchen. He was always looking for something different to offer his customers. Regrettably, we don't know exactly what he did with it, but he probably made a whale meat soup or salad and chowder.

Pop was always concerned about having enough abalone for his restaurant and other abalone ventures. In 1925, he purchased a large piece of property in the Big Sur area, about fifty miles south of Monterey, called Anderson Creek. He learned that abalone are very fertile and will produce millions of eggs when they spawn. He wanted to build an abalone farm to propagate his own abalone. He was so enthusiastic that he got the attention of both the United States government and California Department of Fish & Game, both of which gave him permission build his farm. He also got the attention of some biologists who were interested in his idea. Unfortunately, he was never able to make his farm produce. Abalone reproduce by something called broadcasting—in the wild, the female will release millions of eggs into the ocean, and the male can release trillions of sperm, but getting them to spawn in tanks proved impossible. He didn't have the technology or really the biological know-how at that time.

The idea was a good one, though; he was a man way ahead of his time. After Pop's attempt in 1925, it would be more than forty years before someone else tried raising abalone in California. The Pacific Mariculture Company, run by a man named George Lockwood, started growing abalone in 1966 at Pigeon Point in Santa Cruz County. And in 1968, it sold ten thousand farm-raised red abalone to the Oregon Fish Commission. The company eventually changed its name to the Monterey Abalone Farm, and in 1970, it moved into an abandoned warehouse on Cannery Row. It moved once again in the mid-1980s to Hawaii, where the company operated for about five years. Due to financial issues, it went out of business. But because of Pop's early efforts and the work of George Lockwood and a California Department of Fish & Game biologist named Earl Ebert, after twenty years of experimentation, techniques were developed for spawning and growing red abalone in a farm environment that really kick-started the California abalone industry.

DANCING ON THE BELLY OF THE SHARK

Always looking for ways to market his restaurant, in the summer of 1924, Pop had the idea to take the Hotel Del Monte guests out on Pop's brand-new forty-foot abalone boat, the *Pop Ernest*, where for fifty cents they could harpoon a basking shark. For some unknown reason, beginning in the early 1920s, basking sharks, the second-largest fish in the world, came into Monterey

Bay in very large numbers, sometimes in the hundreds. These sharks can be twenty-five to thirty (and even, in some cases, forty) feet long and were a nuisance to fishermen, often getting tangled in their nets. Pop's partner in this new venture was a Monterey blacksmith named Henry Leppert, who

"Pop's boat." Pop had this small galleon made of concrete and used it as a planter in front of his restaurant. The concrete galleon outlasted Pop, and his restaurant, by many years. Children visiting the wharf would play on it up into the mid-1970s. Circa 1929. *Pat Sands Collection.*

Large basking shark on the beach near the Monterey Wharf. Note you can see the Monterey Wharf in the background. Circa 1909. *City of Monterey, California History Room.*

Monterey Bay basking shark fisherman Freemen "Whitey" Arbo getting ready to harpoon a basking shark. Circa 1948. *City of Monterey, California History Room.*

was born of French parents in Monterey in the latter part of the nineteenth century. As a young man, he apprenticed with a local blacksmith, and while still in his teens, he opened his own smithy shop. Much of Henry's work was with the Monterey Japanese abalone industry, where he made diving shoes, abalone pries and knives. It was through the abalone industry that he first met Pop Ernest.

At that time, there wasn't a market for the basking shark, so Pop and Henry came up with this idea of taking tourists out to harpoon them for sport. Still living in Monterey was a number of retired Portuguese whalers. Pop had arranged to have these whalers come out on his boat to demonstrate how to throw the harpoon and tell their tales of whaling on the Monterey Bay. Pop and Henry were the first to take tourists out on the bay to harpoon basking sharks for sport. At first, they used an old harpoon that Pop had picked up at Point Lobos. It came from a schooner that was once used to smuggle Chinese laborers into California. The ship had burned some years before in Whalers Cove. Henry Leppert began making his own harpoons, though, and soon everyone wanted one of Henry's, as his harpoons were considered to be the best. Initially, they only advertised this "adventure" through the Hotel Del Monte, but it was a big hit. Not only did it attract the average guest, but it also piqued the interest of many well-known writers and artists of the day, such as authors Gouverneur Morris (great-grandson of the Founding Father) and Irvin Cobb. It also attracted royalty, including Count Carzelle of Rome and Lord and Lady Hastings of Great Britain. S.F.B. Morris, president of Del Monte Properties, and artist Jo Mora were also regulars. Both Jo Mora and his son, Jo Jr., were avid hunters and frequent guests on these basking shark excursions. Eventually, Jo and Pop became very close friends.

Because the main purpose of the *Pop Ernest* was collecting abalone, it had an air compressor on board for the divers. Oftentimes, after the kill of a basking shark, Henry Leppert would pump the carcass of the animal with air and then spin it until it was belly-up. He would then get on the dead shark's belly and dance for all the customers. It was a highlight of the trip.

By 1925, there were other companies offering basking shark hunts on the bay, in particular the boat *Two Brothers*, owned and operated by partners Bert Korf and Chester Gilkey. They were only charging twenty-five cents to harpoon a basking shark. Although they didn't offer old whalers as guides aboard their boat, they did have Thomas Machado, son and grandson of Monterey Portuguese whalers, born in Monterey. By the time Thomas came of age, the whaling industry in Monterey had ended, so the opportunity to be part of the basking shark fishing industry, at least for Thomas, was a continuation of the family tradition. He was the first to harpoon sharks systematically and was considered by far the best harpoonist working the bay. There was a day in 1936 when he harpooned six basking sharks in two and a half hours off Del Monte Beach, all with the same harpoon. He holds the 1928 record for the largest shark ever caught, at 8,600 pounds, including a liver that weighed 2,100 pounds. Thomas Machado continued fishing basking sharks into the early 1950s.

The *Two Brothers* was a converted fifty-foot navy motor sailer and could take several passengers at a time. Because this was a tourist-generated industry, the two men were always looking for new ways to entertain their customers. From time to time, they would even jump on the sharks and ride them like bucking broncos at the rodeo. Unfortunately for the rider, the

Large basking shark on the beach near the Monterey Wharf. Circa 1928. *City of Monterey, California History Room.*

basking shark's skin is very rough, almost like little teeth, and it usually tore the rider's legs up.

When Pop and Henry Leppert started their fishery in 1924, it was strictly for sport and to promote his restaurant. The usual practice was to leave the dead shark to the elements out on the bay. But beginning in 1927, there was a new player in town named Max Schaefer. Schaefer was in the reduction business. He had a small plant out in the sand dunes in Seaside. He worked with the sardine industry, buying whole fish from the fishermen. Before 1929, there was no "official" sardine season. Sardines were fished whenever they came into the bay. The reduction process was simple, requiring fewer than five employees to run the plant, and it was very profitable. For Schaefer, the primary market was the chicken industry—they produced cheap chicken feed from the offal of the Monterey sardine. The next time you go to the store and buy a chicken, you can thank the Monterey sardine. Before 1920, the chicken industry in California was not doing well. People didn't eat chicken like we do today because it was expensive. They began to produce this cheap chicken feed out of the Monterey canneries, and the chickens thrived on it. Because of that, more and more chickens were produced, and the prices went down. When prices dropped, people began to buy them. The California chicken industry was saved by the bones of the Monterey sardine.

Schaefer couldn't help but notice all the basking shark activity and thought that he could do something with them. He began to buy the carcasses from the "fishermen." His plan was to grind them up for dog and cat food and use the oil from the livers for a product he called "Sun Shark Liver Oil: Nature's Own Tonic." The oil from the basking shark is a low-grade vitamin A and really isn't good for much, but his brochure proclaimed:

> *Made from the livers of the Sun or Basking Shark only. It is used as a tonic to build up the digestive system, enabling it to get out all nutrients contained in regular food…It is giving relief in cases of neuritis, stomach ulcers, anemia, loss of appetite and weight, lack of energy, asthmatic attacks and has also in several cases reduced and finally eliminated the growth of goiters. It promotes health and growth in children, builds up resistance to attacks of the usual ailments of youth and furnishes energy for the strenuous exertions of youth…In older people it is deferring troubles common with age, enables them to keep on enjoying their full bodily vigor and energy to perform their daily task.*

It sold very well, and there was money to be made. Soon there were several basking shark fishermen working the bay. At first, Schaefer was paying ten dollars per ton, but by 1933, he was paying as much as twenty dollars per ton. Considering that a basking shark can weigh as much as eight thousand pounds, and that it was possible to bring in more than one a day, that was pretty good money. This continued until 1938, when Max Schaefer's reduction plant burned to the ground.

"ART COLONY" ON THE WHARF

Just like his old restaurant on Alvarado Street, his new "Pop" Ernest restaurant on the Monterey Wharf attracted the art community. Regulars included poets George Sterling and Charles Warren Stoddard; writer Jimmy Hopper; and painters Charles Rollo Peters, Armin Hansen, Evelyn McCormick, Isabelle Hunter, E. Charlton Fortune and Jo Mora. These

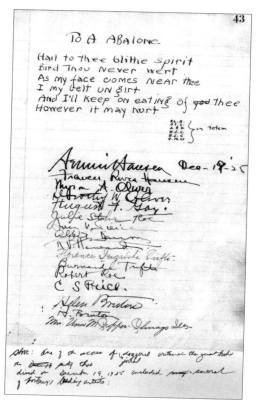

Left: A page from the guest book signed by several noted Monterey artists, including Armin Hansen, Myron Oliver, August Gay, Julie Stohr, Lucy Pierce and Helen Burton. Pop's was a favorite place for many of Monterey's art community. This page dates to December 19, 1925. *Pat Sands Collection.*

Below: This famous menu was given away as a souvenir. The artwork was a collaborative effort by two well-known Monterey artists: Jo Mora, who did the middle section, and Armin Hansen, who did the outside borders. Mora and Hansen did the menu for free abalone dinners. Circa 1930. *Author's collection.*

Opposite: Famed silent movie comedian Charlie Chaplin is gazing out at the Monterey Harbor as Pop stands behind him. Circa 1930. *Pat Sands Collection.*

artists would often paint Pop and his restaurant, and the finished painting would end up hanging on the walls of the restaurant.

Jo Mora and Armin Hansen teamed up to create the artwork for a menu that would be given out as a souvenir. Each artist took a different section of this colorful menu. Jo Mora created the middle section, which featured a caricature of Pop holding a frying pan over a fire while fish are jumping out of a fish bowl into the hot pan. There are seahorse waiters, waving abalone and shoe-wearing lobsters. Hansen created the border section, which has a beautiful, stylized octopus in the right corner, with its tentacles stretching across the front and down the side. He wrote, "Complements of Pop Ernest" on top, replacing the *C* in "Complements" and the *P* in

"Pop" and the *E* in "Ernest" with fish as letters. At the bottom of the menu, Hansen wrote, "Abalone Sea Food Restaurant, Auf Wiedersehen," again using fish to replace the first letters and incorporating the German phrase for "until we meet again." Mora and Hansen's payment for the artwork were free abalone dinners. But it wasn't just artists and writers; there were other celebrities as well, like Charles Lindbergh, who was in Monterey in March 1930 to demonstrate flying a glider. Silent film stars like Charlie Chaplin, Fatty Arbuckle and Mabel Normand ate abalone for the first time in Pop's restaurant, as did Clark Gable, Barbara Stanwyck, Claudette Colbert, John Garfield and a number of other Hollywood celebrities.

TRAGEDY AND CHALLENGES

Along with Pop's success and acclaim came tragedy. On May 6, 1928, Pop's youngest son, Otto, committed suicide; he shot himself twice in the head with a handgun. He was just twenty-seven years of age. It's always been a mystery, even in the Doeltar family, as to why Otto killed himself; he didn't leave a note. Unlike today, in 1928, there wasn't a lot of support for someone suffering from depression. He didn't have that lifeline; he didn't even know how to reach for it. Some even thought that it may have been an accident. The family didn't really talk about it much. The night before Otto's death, he and his wife, Mabel, attended a dance at the Stickers Hall in Monterey, a popular place that was frequented by many who worked in the Monterey restaurant business, and by all accounts had good time. Otto's two sons, Robert and Fred, who were very young, were Pop's favorite grandkids. Family was very important to Pop. He always wanted everyone to be close. It was a difficult time for the whole Doelter family, but especially for Pop, who never really got over Otto's death.

Pop's biggest concern, as noted, was getting fresh abalone on a consistent basses. His abalone farm didn't pan out; it was just too many years before its time, and his dive crew couldn't always get enough abalone for the restaurant. So, he had to buy abalone from other sources on the Monterey Wharf. Abalone diver Roy Hattori's mother ran an abalone processing plant just across from the restaurant in the Booth's cannery, and she was contracted to produce special large abalone steaks for Pop. But he continued to complain about getting fresh abalone. He felt that the abalone was being

The restaurant. Note that you can still read "Boats for Hire" on the roof. Circa 1920. *Pat Sands Collection.*

overfished and that there were not enough controls in the industry. In 1929, 3.4 million pounds of abalone were unloaded at the Monterey Wharf. N.B. Schofield, head of the Marine Division for the California Department of Fish & Game, announced in 1929 that the fishery was healthy and that the "laws protecting the abalone are ideal, and it is not likely fishermen will deplete the supply." Pop was incensed and wrote a letter to the *Monterey Herald* on September 14, 1929:

> *Open letter regarding the statement of Mr. N.B. Schofield of the State Fish and Game Commission that "Laws protecting the abalone are ideal, and it is not likely fishermen will deplete the supply." Some of the laws, as I understand them are as follows (and they are indeed ideal).*
>
> *1. Abalone can only be used for food purposes.*
> *2. Abalone must be brought ashore alive in their shells and must conform to a certain size.*
> *3. Abalone cannot be shipped out of the State of California.*

4. Crews of boats gathering abalone must be composed of one-half U.S. white citizens.

But the following conditions in the abalone industry come first hand to my attention every day, and a survey easily by the commission world easily verify them.

It is a well-known fact that abalone in Monterey county is completely fished out, and the abalone that is being brought in from San Luis Obispo county is in such a state that a staggering amount has to be discarded and goes into fertilizer.

The boats are out three and sometimes four days, and, it is five days between the time some of the abalones are taken from the water and the time they are handled by the packers on the wharf at Monterey. To this length of time the abalone is out of the water can be laid the blame for the deplorable condition that the abalone is arriving daily into this port. This could be remedied by having the abalones put into water-liters immediately upon being taken from the water, and they can be kept alive in this condition for quite awhile.

People coming to my place of business and with whom I come into contact from all cities in the United States, complain to me that the frozen abalones they get from California are tasteless and tough; and it stands to reason that the abalones as they are packed are unfit for food for man's consumption. If the law, as it is, could be enforced, there could be no abalone consigned to fertilizer, nor would there be any complaint of their being tasteless.

The laws are absolutely protective to the abalone industry, but the laws are not enforced.

Signed: Ernest (Pop) Doelter.

He wrote this letter, in part, because he believed that the fishery could be depleted and also because he was concerned about competition. More and more restaurants that featured abalone were opening in California, and by 1929, the majority of the businesses on the Monterey Wharf were Japanese fish markets and abalone processors, selling their product to the same hotels and restaurants as Pop. He was also wrong in some of his facts. Just two days later, in the *Monterey Herald*, J.A. Zanetta, manager of the A. Paladini Company, a large fish processor with plants in San Francisco and Monterey, responded with this letter:

"ERNEST" OR "ERNST"?

Zanetta Answers Abalone Epistle

My Dear Sir:

After reading Ernest (Pop) Doelter's letter on your issue of September 14, relative to the method of gathering and preparing abalone by different packers on the municipal wharf at Monterey I was somewhat incensed at the misstatements he has made in the article you have published over his caption. For your information and the information of your readers, we will tell you the true facts as exist in our method of taking abalone and preparing them for marketing, but first we will try and answer a few of the erroneous assertions that Ernest (Pop) Doelter, has made in his letter.

No. 1 Abalone can only be used for food purposes; this is correct provided, however, it is received by the packer in a condition making it fit for human consumption.

No. 2 Abalones must be brought to the shore alive and attached to the shell and must conform to a certain size. (Absolutely correct.)

No. 3 Abalones cannot be shipped out of the State. (Once more he goes to the head of the class; correct).

No. 4 Crews of boats gathering abalone must be comprised of one-half white U.S. citizens. (Very wrong; we have never been able to find anything in the statutes of California that made any distinction as to nationality regarding fishing crews.)

Regarding his assertion that abalones are entirely fished out in Monterey County, again he is mistaken; such is not the fact. It is true that the concerns interested in the packing of abalone had at last session of the state legislature a district opened in San Luis Obispo county to commercial abalone fishing in order to increase our supply to meet the constant growing demand for this delicious and palatable sea food, the district we were confined to in former years having been heavily fished but by no means depleted of abalone and if necessary our crews could go into the old district and still gather large quantities of abalone, but for the good of the industry we deem it advisable to give the old fishing ground a rest and take our supply from the new district just opened up, for the balance of the present season. Abalone fishing is somewhat like farming, the beds have to be cultivated the same as a lettuce crop; in other words if abalones are not thinned out the same as lettuce where they are too thick it allows no room for expansion and furthermore the food supply is not adequate to cope with the situation and the result is a crop of thin and dead abalones that are found on the bottom by divers and never taken but are allowed to remain where found. Relative to the condition that they brought into the wharf at Monterey and the staggering amount that goes to the reduction plants the facts are that we send all the offal and trimmings of the abalone to the reduction plant, but as to whole or good abalone going to the reduction plant that is absolutely false. By offal we mean the entrails of abalone which cannot be used for anything else and the trimmings of the abalone that is cut from the edges of the abalone and the skin. These trimmings we have never been able to find a market for and if anyone can utilize them whereby they can be made fit for human consummation we will gladly give them to them for hauling of them away. As to their being an elapsed time of from four to five days between the gathering and the delivering of abalone to the packers, again he is wrong; for your information our crews leave here taking one day to run to the fishing ground and two days to fish, returning the night of the second day's fishing, allowing the diving crews to deliver their abalones to us in a live state and we immediately go to work preparing them for shipment, as if allowed to die on our hands we would be forced to sustain severe losses. It is true that in a large load of abalone and extremely hot weather we may have one or two dozen dead abalones which we do not prepare but are given to the poor or anyone who cares to take them for nothing, but never do we send any whole abalone to the reduction plant. As to using water liters to the abalones more alive we tried this experiment some years ago back and found it impractical as it had a tendency to kill the abalone instead of reviving it so we discontinued the practice. As to the people coming from cities throughout the United States and complaining about the frozen abalones they receive from California being tasteless and tough, this is not true as we are not allowed to ship abalones out of the state of California and the Fish and Game commission and their deputies make their business to see that we do not violate the law. As to enforcement of the fish and game laws here at Monterey we can only say that while we are not in the fish business to succeed by law violation, yet it would be folly for us to try to do so as the deputies of the Fish and Game commission are constantly on the job attending to their duties, and in many instances we believe a little too drastic on minor violations. As to abalones being tough after they have been prepared by the different packers, we can only say that they have been made tough in the cooking. Abalone if overcooked will become tough and tasteless; this is something over which we have no control.

To start an agitation to have a law enacted to do away with the commercializing of the abalone would be an injustice to every merchant *in this town, as facts and figures will show that there is approximately $1,000,000,00 spent in the abalone industry annually of which approximately 75 percent remains in Monterey.*

This remarkable letter, although a bit condescending, was correct. I'm sure that Zanetta's letter upset Pop; after all, he was the "Abalone King." More importantly, none of these other abalone companies would have existed without Pop and the recipe that he developed way back in 1908.

ALL THOSE ABALONE SHELLS

With each boat coming into Monterey with upward of two hundred dozen large red abalone, there were a lot of shells. Pop would just give them away, and people would embed them into walls or fireplaces, and still today there

Pop on the Monterey Wharf with a large pile of abalone shells. He would just give these shells away. A lot of Monterey gardens still have abalone shell borders, and people would embed the shells into their concrete walls. All thanks to Pop. Circa 1925. *Pat Sands Collection.*

are many gardens on the Monterey Peninsula that are lined with abalone shell that they got from Pop. They would also just truck them out to Seaside, where there were lots of sand dunes, and just dump them. Abalone diver Roy Hattori remembered:

> *We took those shells by the thousands and trucked 'em out to Seaside, just about where the Beach Hotel is, and just dumped them on the dunes there. And there must have been…everybody dumped their shells out there. I don't know how many shells there were, just thousands and thousands. 'Cause each time they were operating out of Monterey, and each boat would get somewhere in the neighborhood of two hundred dozen in a trip. They all went out at the same time, and just about all came back at the same time. So at one time on the wharf, there would be two thousand dozen abalone. Each boat would carry about two hundred dozen, and there were ten boats. So ten times two hundred is two thousands—two thousand dozen abalone at one time on the wharf. And everybody…all the Japanese community and a lot of the Italian people would come down and process 'em. And so all those shells all went out to Seaside.*

Sometime in the late 1920s, there was a company from Torrance, California, called Salm that would come to Monterey and collect all of those abalone shells (filling up train cars), take the shells back to Torrance and produce trinkets that were sold at tourist attractions all over the United States. These trinkets were made of Monterey red abalone shells that were cut into shapes like anchors, hatchets, cribbage boards, fish, salt and pepper shakers and more. This author has one shaped like the state of North Dakota and then glued onto a piece of cut redwood. Each knickknack had a thermometer glued to the front and the name of the town or place where they were being sold—like Key West, Florida; Atlanta, Georgia; or Akron, Ohio; nothing says *Ohio* like abalone! These wonderful gewgaws usually came in a box tied down with a piece of thread ready to be mailed to that special person. Due to the popularity of these abalone products, the Salm Company in 1928 had to expand its factory. In a story that appeared in the *Torrance Herald* on February 9, 1928:

> FINE NEW LINE ADDED
> *New Abalone Shell Products Gain Widespread Favor in. U.S.*
>
> *Increased production due to widespread demand for all of its products and the addition of a new line of abalone shell articles has prompted the Salm*

Manufacturing Company to make plans for a 25 percent increase in its floor space in its plant in Torrance. John Salm, president of the company, has placed on the market an attractive new line of abalone shell picture frames, salt and pepper shakers, cake knives, fruit sets, table lamps and candle holders. Salm knives and manicure sets are the most widely known abalone shell products in the country. For the past few years the Torrance plant has been operating at capacity to satisfy the demand. The new line of goods has met with widespread favor all over the country according to Mr. Salm, who recently returned from a trip to the East. The Salm Manufacturing Company is the largest user of abalone shells in the United States.

And almost all that abalone shell came from Monterey!

Later, in the late 1940s, a Monterey company called Couroc began to make beautiful inlayed trays out of a heavy plastic utilizing those same red abalone shells for the inlay.

The whole Ernest family was involved in the restaurant and lived within one block of one another and in walking distance to the Monterey Wharf. By 1921, most of the Doelter kids, except Carl, were married and had children of their own. Pop no longer worked in the kitchen, with the exception of preparing all the abalone for cooking, Pop Ernest style, every morning. He could usually be found out front greeting all his guests. He really was a larger-than-life character, weighing close to three hundred pounds; with his white apron, chef's coat and red fez, as well as that goatee and mustache, he looked very mysterious. And people from all walks of life, the rich and the poor, came to meet him.

Pop on the Monterey Wharf walking one of his German Shepherds. Pop loved animals, especially his two dogs. Circa 1928. *Pat Sands Collection.*

Above: Pop sitting with an unknown customer. Note that she's enjoying Pop's abalone stew, which was served in the abalone shell. Circa 1925. *Pat Sands Collection.*

Left: Pop serving his abalone stew to two unknown customers. Circa 1925. *Pat Sands Collection.*

And he always had a good word for everyone. He would often invite young soldiers and those who may have been a little short in the pocketbook to "have a meal on me."

When the Depression hit in 1930, business slowed down. And Prohibition was still in effect, so they couldn't serve liquor, and that hurt. Luckily, they still had a loyal following, particularly with the locals, who would come to have an abalone dinner and spend time talking with Pop. And, of course, he had the Hotel Del Monte crowd, who would come to Monterey and make it a point to eat at Pop's. One of items that people came for the most was his famous abalone stew. This creamy stew, made with abalone, potatoes, celery, onion, milk, butter and abalone nectar, was served in the abalone shell. The holes of the shell were filled with lead.

In April 1930, A.M. Allan, owner of Point Lobos and partner to Gennosuke Kodani, died. Allan was more than just a business partner to Kodani; they were friends. Because Allan saw the potential in the abalone fishery, he was able to provide much-needed jobs for many Japanese fishermen who came to Monterey. These fishermen were sending money home that kept

Pop Ernest's Restaurant. Note the painted octopus on the front wall. Circa 1940. *Pat Sands Collection.*

Passport photo of Ernest "Pop" Doelter. Circa 1930. *Pat Sands Collection.*

their families alive. Allan also opened a sardine cannery on present-day Cannery Row called the Monterey Canning Company in 1917, employing a number of Japanese workers. Because of A.M. Allan's unfailing friendship and support of Gennosuke Kodani and of the Japanese community, and especially the fishermen of Chiba, Japan, a memorial service was held for him at the Chosho-ji Temple in Chikura, Japan, on April 24, 1930. Attending were many fishermen who had fished and dived for abalone in Monterey Bay. And just a few months later, on July 1, 1930, Gennosuke Kodani died. He was just sixty-three years of age. The following year, the Point Lobos Abalone Company closed. But because of Pop's recipe, there was still a big demand for abalone, and there were several Japanese abalone companies working off the Monterey Wharf.

On March 22, 1933, President Franklin Roosevelt signed the Cullen-Harrison Act, allowing for the first time in thirteen years the manufacture and sale of beer and wine in the United States. The complete repeal of Prohibition would not take effect until December 5, 1933. When "beer came back," Pop was granted the first beer license by the City of Monterey. He went to work to celebrate this happy occasion, and on June 4, 1933, he opened his new taproom. He insisted that it was not a beer garden but merely an improvement "to make my guests more comfortable." He spent about $5,000 on improvements, inclosing the open porch with a roof and large glass windows overlooking the bay. It was decorated like the larger restaurant in a nautical theme, with fish baskets, shells and carved wood beams. And just like his earlier Ernest's Tavern, which he opened in 1909, all the beer was served in German beer steins. On the day of the opening of the new bar, he brought in a small orchestra to entertain his guests. A story about the opening appeared the next day in the *Monterey Herald* that featured a photo of a smiling Pop holding a large, foaming beer stein. The word "Gesundheit" ("health" in German) was printed above the photo.

SUNNYBOY

Pop's biggest competition on the Monterey Wharf was a restaurant called the Pilot Seafood Restaurant, which opened in February 1933 in a building just directly across from Pop Ernest. It was owned and operated by a man described as "a colorful Greek" named George "Sunnyboy" Vellis. The Pilot was famous for its clams and eastern-style oysters, but he also sold abalone. The Pilot quickly became a popular place, taking some of Pop's customers with it.

Sunnyboy first came to Monterey in 1927 and opened a fish market on the Monterey Wharf. When the stock market crashed in 1929, he lost his market. Sunnyboy was quoted as saying, "When my partners Giannini and J.P. Morgan sold me out back on Wall Street, I had to leave the fish market." Luckily for Sunnyboy, a wealthy friend helped him out, and he was able to open the Pilot. Two weeks later, the banks closed. When he closed the restaurant in 1953, the *Monterey Herald* ran a story about him, and this is what he said about those times: "Those were rough days, millionaires were selling apples and only the coffin business was booming. They were all jumping out of windows in those days. I weathered okay but I did just about everything except jump out of a window." It's never been clear why he was called Sunnyboy, but he always said that he got the name from a Monterey merchant named Elmer Zanetta but wouldn't reveal why he called him that.

One of Vellis's regular customers was the writer John Steinbeck, who, according to Vellis, wrote much of the book *Cannery Row* in the restaurant. Sunnyboy could point to a particular corner in the restaurant where Steinbeck would sit and write "over a bottle of brandy, over many bottles of brandy." He also became a character in Steinbeck's follow-up to *Cannery Row*, *Sweet Thursday*. Steinbeck described Sunnyboy in *Sweet Thursday* in the chapter "One Night of Love":

> *Sunny Boy is truly the only Greek born in America named Sunny Boy. He operates a restaurant and bar on the wharf, in Monterey. Sunny Boy*

is plump and getting plumper. Although he was born near Sutro Park in San Francisco, and went to public schools, Sunny Boy has singlehandedly kept alive the Near East. His perfectly round face hints Orient Express and beautiful spies. His bush voice is congenitally confidential. Sunny Boy can say "good evening" and make sound like an international plot. His restaurant makes friends for him and supports him. Perhaps Sunny Boy, in one sense, wears a long black cape and dines with Balkan countesses where two seas kiss the Golden Horn—but he also runs a good restaurant. He probably knows more secrets than any man in the community, for his martinis are a combination truth serum and lie detector.

Later in the 1940s, when the sardine fishery was still going strong, Sunnyboy hung two large brass keys over his bar. He said, "Those were the keys to the sardine business. Before long, they'll be used to lock up all those fish plants."

With the end of Prohibition in December 1933, the restaurant could add mixed drinks to the bar menu. Everyone who worked in the restaurant learned to mix drinks. According to older son Carl, it was mostly Manhattans, martinis and highballs. And mixed drinks were only served to the guests who were eating in the restaurant. Pop was not interested in creating a bar trade. He didn't consider his beer bar or taproom to be bars. Pop would tell those looking just for drinks, "The town is full of bars; go find one."

Pop was always a big man. At one point, he weighed close to three hundred pounds; he always enjoyed a good meal. By 1934, his health was beginning to deteriorate, and he spent more time at home and less time at the restaurant. He made a trip to Gilroy to see an old friend who was a doctor, who told him that "there is nothing I can do for you." Carl and Mother Vera took Pop to see another in doctor in Monterey, and the news was not good. He had stomach and liver cancer. Pop never knew what was wrong with him; the doctor only shared his diagnosis with Carl and Vera, and they chose not to tell him.

Even though he was in severe pain, Pop could be found every evening sitting on the porch of the restaurant, greeting his guests and welcoming them to Pop Ernest's. Finally, in November of that same year, he stopped going to the restaurant altogether, allowing Carl and Ernest Jr. to take control. He passed away in the early morning hours of December 28, 1934, with his beloved Vera, Carl and Ernest Jr. at his bedside. Obituaries for Pop appeared in newspapers across the nation, from New York to San Diego and almost every small town in between. They all had a similar theme to this one from the *Monterey Herald*:

"ERNEST" OR "ERNST"?

Famous Restaurateur Was Discover of Abalone

One of Monterey's most colorful figures and a master of cuisine with an international reputation died today, Associated Press dispatches report. He was Ernest Doelter, known to epicures everywhere as "Pop" Ernest the man who made abalone famous.

The death of Pop Ernest on Monterey meant the passing of an institution for the huge benevolent, fezz-hatted man was all of that. He and his little restaurant perched on piles on fishermen's wharf at Monterey were a landmarks not only of the seaport town that was California's first capital, but of the Pacific Coast as well. Books written about the famous chefs and dinning places of the world speak with respect pf the man who died today and of the restaurant he founded.

The man credited with having taught Californians abalone was something to eat and not just a seashell died today. He was Ernest (Pop) Doelter Waterfront restaurant man. He came from Baden, Germany, 50 years ago and was regarded as the founder of the state's abalone industry.

Pop Ernest made a picturesque sight. His body was of ample girth. His sweeping mustaches and goatee somehow were reminiscent of Buffalo Bill. His blue eyes were twinkling and kind. He took an affectionate interest in his guests, among whose tables he moved with a slow and impressive walk. It was an affection that was always returned.

I think Pop would have been proud. I know his family was. It was a large funeral, and family and friends came from all over to attend, including politicians, businessmen, artists, the rich and the poor. Pop had somehow touched them all. He left an estate worth $100,000, about $1 million today. Abalone was very good to him.

The demand for fresh abalone, not just in Monterey but everywhere, continued to get bigger. By 1934, there was a real push to open the bay again for commercial abalone fishing, it having been closed for commercial use since 1899. The California Department of Fish & Game supported the reopening of the bay, as did a number of marine biologists who all said that it was healthy and sustainable. A bill was being sent through the California state legislature to open the bay from the Carmel River to the Monterey Wharf. The expected pushback, coming mostly from the hunting and sport fishing community, came fast and hard. Mr. W.R. Holman, who was an avid sportsman and owner of the largest department store in Monterey County, Holman's Department Store (the Holman family has a long history on

BILL OF FARE

COCKTAILS

Oyster	30c	Crab	30c
Lobster	40c	Shrimp	30c

SOUPS

Abalone Chowder	25c
Abalone Nectar	25c
Clam Chowder	25c

SALADS

Crab Salad	75c	Crab Louis	90c
Lobster Salad	90c	Lobster Louis	90c
Shrimp Salad	75c	Sliced Tomatoes	20c
Lettuce and Tomatoes	20c	Lettuce	15; (two) 25c

FISH
Fresh Daily

Filet of Abalone, Tartar Sauce			1.25
Fried Shrimps			75
Lobster, Tartar Sauce			75c and $1.00
Filet of Sole, Tartar Sauce	70c	Cracked Crab	70c
Oysters, fried	75c	Halibut	70c
Mackerel	65c	Sea Bass	70c
Salmon	70c	Rockcod	65c
Sandabs	65c	Scallops	75c

POTATOES

French Fried		15c; (two) 25c
Lyonnaise	20c	
Saute Hashed Brown		20c

DESSERTS

French Pancake	50c	With Rum	75c

BEVERAGES

Coffee	10c	Tea (pot)	15c	Milk	10c

A Single Portion Served for Two Persons - - 25c Extra Charge

"All prices listed are ceiling prices unless otherwise indicated, in which case they are below ceiling prices. By OPA regulations our ceiling prices are our highest prices from April 4, 1943 to April 10, 1943. Records of these are available for your inspection."

Menu prices. You can date the menu by the prices for the abalone steak. This one dates to circa 1935; the abalone steak dinner was $1.25.

the Monterey Peninsula and a lot of political clout), was asked to make a response on behalf of the sporting community. He wrote a letter to George D. Northenholt, director of California's Natural Resources Division. The rather long letter gives a brief history of the Monterey abalone fishery, especially the Japanese abalone fishery, as well as some natural history of the abalone. He also included this in his letter:

> *Mr. "Pop" Ernest operated a Fish Grotto close to the Custom House in Monterey, which was famous from Coast to Coast, owned his own diving outfit and employed his own divers, and had made a study of abalone life and habits for many years.*
>
> *Less than two months previous to his death he called at my office and explained to me that a movement was on foot for opening the district between the Monterey Wharf and Carmel River. He did not state, however, just what methods were to be used to open this district, but implored of me when the time came that I use every effort to prevent the opening of this district to abalone fishing. He made this statement that the territory covered by this reserve was so open, without crevices or places for the abalones to hide, that within less than three weeks every available abalone within commercial size would be taken from our shores, and leave Monterey County without any reserve spawning grounds whatsoever.*
>
> *He also explained that up to about a year back his diving crews had no trouble in going out and getting boatloads of abalones, but that the condition had entirely changed and that many times his divers would come back with not over a dozen abalones. I am sure that his sons, who are now in charge of the business, as Mr. "Pop" Ernst* [sic] *has passed on, will verify this condition.*

He also made this remarkable observation about the abalone:

> *The abalones do not remain stationary, as stated by some of our professors, and of our Commissioners. Schools of abalone travel with the tide back and forth, the same as fish. I have, personally, before the limit, years back filled barley sacks with abalones, as they were swimming through the water like fish* [abalone do not swim], *and have the actual proof of this condition, as others were with me gathering them as they were coming in with the tide.*

I'm not sure what Holman was talking about when he wrote about seeing "swimming abalone." I've talked to a number of marine biologists who work with abalone about this phenomenon, and they were skeptical to say the least. He ended his letter with this:

> *For your information I wish to state that requests to the Governor to veto this bill have been made by the Pacific Grove Council, by Mayor Sheldon Gilmer, by the Junior Chamber of Commerce of Monterey, by the Chamber of Commerce of Pacific Grove, by unanimous vote of the Sportsmen's Clubs of the Monterey Peninsula, in session representing 140 members, by the Lighthouse Club, representing 80 members, by the Lions Club of the Monterey Peninsula, by Reginald Foster, City Attorney for Pacific Grove, by Sportsmen Clubs of Salinas, Watsonville and Santa Cruz, through their representative and by the Chamber of Commerce of Santa Cruz, and if we had the opportunity and time thousands of our residents on the Monterey Peninsula who are vitally interested in preserving the abalones would flood the Governor's office with protests against the opening of this territory.*
>
> *Yours very sincerely,*
> *W.R. Holman*
> *Monterey Peninsula Sportsmen's Conservation Club*

The abalone fishing district from the Carmel River to the Monterey Wharf has never been reopened.

Carl and Ernest Jr. continued to run the restaurant as Pop would have, and initially business was good, but it was the Depression and money was tight. So, they decided to eliminate the diving operations and buy fresh abalone from one of the many abalone processors already on the Monterey Wharf. Since they were no longer in the diving business, they were also no longer in the abalone brokering business. All their concentration was focused on the restaurant. Besides the cooking, Ernest Jr. was also the bookkeeper and Carl the headwaiter. Mother Vera would fill in as hostess, but her health was failing. On June 16, 1937, she passed away at home with daughter Minnie at her side.

As the '30s moved into the '40s, more restaurants and seafood stands opened on the Monterey Wharf and around the peninsula; each new restaurant featured some type of abalone dish on its menu—abalone sandwiches were particularly popular. But most of the abalone being served was Pop Ernest style. And as it turns out, there was a market for the trimmings, or the mantel, in spite of what J.A. Zanetta wrote in his letter the *Monterey Herald* back in 1929. All those trimmings were being pressed

Pop Ernest's Restaurant. Circa 1940. *Pat Sands Collection.*

into a patty, like a hamburger patty, and sold in grocery stores and small markets around the peninsula. This was a very inexpensive way to enjoy abalone. To combat the new competition, Carl and Ernest Jr. began to call their restaurant the "originators of abalone sea foods." And Ernest Jr. became "Pop" Ernest Jr. But business continued to fall off, especially in the winter months, to the point that the restaurant wasn't profitable.

By 1940, most of the Monterey divers from Japan had returned home, mainly because of food and supply shortages due to rationing. There a few exceptions, like the Kodani family, who were already established here. There was also a diver named Tajuro Watanabe, who was the owner of his own abalone boat called the *Empress.* Mr. Watanabe also worked with Roy Hattori in his abalone operation. The last diver to leave Point Lobos was Gennosuke Takahashi, who did not return to Japan until after World War II, spending the war in an internment camp. He finally went home in December 1947.

Also in 1940, the United States government transferred the customhouse and surrounding area, including the property where the restaurant stood, to the State of California to develop as a park. The deed stipulated that "there shall be no private enterprises within the limits." If the restaurant were not removed, the property would revert back the federal government. In a 1940 editorial in the *Monterey Herald*, the writer said, in part:

> *Traditions will cling to the shores and weather-beaten boards. Legal questions aimed to give us for perpetuity lands loved in our story, threaten to remove an "intrusion" which on its own, won favor and fame. The old Ernst or "Ernest" place, with its memories of Stevenson, Sterling, Stoddard and the rest, is ruled out by law. As it was threatened by decay and met with a challenge for modernization which would rob it of its appeal, it may be as well. More of the original setting of the Custom House is restored: Monterey may still have abalone.*

Luckily, a deal was made between the U.S. government and the state to allow the restaurant to stay. When the orders came down in April 1941 removing the Japanese community from the Monterey Peninsula, Roy Hattori had to sell all his abalone diving gear, including his boats, for pennies on the dollar. He ended up being drafted into the U.S. Army and becoming a member of the Military Intelligence Service (MIS), with which he served in the South Pacific and Japan during the U.S. occupation.

After the war, when Roy returned home to Monterey, he did return to commercial abalone diving, but just for a few years. The industry, at least in the Monterey area, had changed, in part because there just weren't enough abalone to make it viable. But he did become a recreational diver. He liked to free dive, *ama* style, a nod to those who came before him. When asked why he liked to dive without tanks, he said:

> *I just never got used to having a tank on my back. I just wasn't comfortable thinking that I had to depend on a tank for my air, and so I never really went into scuba diving. I just free dove all the time—just held my breath and you can really develop a lot of staying power just by learning to hyperventilate. And I could stay down almost two minutes on a working dive.*
>
> *I did enjoy skin diving. And all the time when I used to dive and used to run the bottom looking for abalone, I used to look around and I'd think if the public could do this, just to see the bottom of the ocean, I'd think, "Gee, what a great thing it would be." And then after the war, along came the Aqua-Lung, and everybody became a diver. But it's such a different world once you get your face under water. And I used to always tell my mother and brother and everybody that, and I'd say, "You know, diving is so different.*

Patricia Doelter, Carl Doelter's daughter, and her mother, Eileen, in front of the restaurant in 1947. *Pat Sands Collection.*

The world is so different under water. And it's so beautiful, there's so many things to see that you could sit by a rock under water and spend a whole day and see something different every minute!"

Pop Ernest's started to close down between November and February, only opening on three-day holiday weekends. From March to May, it would open on Fridays, Saturdays and Sundays if the weather was good. Even though the family had a loyal local following, that wasn't enough to keep the restaurant open. They were so dependent on the tourist and hotel trade to get them through those months. In the summers, they were open every day, and the restaurant was busy almost all the time. The money they made in the summer months was enough to tide them over during slower winter months.

By 1950, Ernest Jr. was having some health issues, and in 1952, the two brothers decided to sell the restaurant to Sal Cerrito for $20,000. The Cerritos, who first came to the peninsula in the mid-1920s, were in the restaurant business on the Monterey Wharf and were, at one point, one of Pop's competitors. The Cerritos had as many as seven restaurants, including Neptune's Table, also on the Wharf. Cerrito remodeled the old restaurant, getting rid of many of the nautical artifacts that had accumulated over the years, including old ship bells, lanterns, ship name boards, life preservers and seashells—things that gave the restaurant its character. Carl and Ernest divided up the paintings, many by well-known Monterey artists, that were traded for meals over the years. They also kept the guest books, with all the famous signatures and the pages and pages of the "abalone song."

The name was changed to "Cerrito's," but to the consternation of Sal Cerrito, most people in Monterey still called it "Pop's." The one constant between Pop Ernest and Cerrito's was Carl. He continued to work as a waiter there. Many of Pop's old customers would come to Cerrito's because Carl was the unifying factor between the old Pop Ernest and the new Cerrito's. Ernest Jr. repaired radios and TVs, more as a hobby than as a vocation. Carl eventually left Cerrito's when they made him a bartender, but he still liked to work special banquets and especially the Bing Crosby Golf Clambake. Both Carl and Ernest Jr. are gone now, Ernest Jr. in 1960 and Carl in 1979, but the legacy continues.

Abalone was a big part of the Cerrito's menu, and although Sal had his own recipes, the menu was still inspired by Pop Ernest. According to the famed Monterey chef John Pisto, who worked for Cerrito's in the mid-1960s:

Sal would buy abalone "center cuts" for $2.50 a pound wholesale. These slices were very thick and the size of a dinner platter. One recipe is to dip in flour and finish dipping in beaten eggs, then grill on a flat top and turn over when the abalone milk shows [when you cook abalone, a white substance will come up that lets you know when to turn]. *Total* *time was about one and a half to two minutes, then they would top it with sliced almonds, sherry, lemon and butter. Another recipe is flour, eggs and fine cracker meal, grill on flat top, lightly brown and serve with lemon. What made these so delicious was that the pieces were ¼-inch thick and probably eight ounces or more. The results were very moist, tender and had that wonderful abalone taste.*

Cerrito's would get its abalone from a processor in Cayucos that would, after getting the abalone out of the shell, place them in a burlap sack and pound the sacks with heavy two-by-fours.

In the late 1950s, the State of California wanted to take over the property and restore the shoreline back to what it would have looked like when Commodore John Drake Sloat's marines landed there on July 7, 1846, and raised the American flag over the customhouse. Cerrito then took the state to court to try and stop this action, but in 1959, the court ruled in favor of the State Division of Parks and Beaches. At this point, the state had two options. It could tear the old restaurant down or move it. Because of financial issues, it chose to tear it down. The City of Monterey, which owned the building, canceled Cerrito's lease, but he continued to pay month to month. The legal wranglings continued for several more years until September 7, 1967, when the state director of parks and recreation, William Penn Mott announced that the state would tear down Cerrito's within two months. Sal was given a date of October 31, 1967, to close the restaurant. But again, Sal got a reprieve through the courts until 1973, when the City of Monterey hired a planner to write an environmental impact report and the Coastal Commission got involved. Things began to heat up, and by this point, the old building was in pretty bad shape and in desperate need of restoration.

As the court proceedings progressed, a fire broke out in the restaurant on September 16, 1975, and burned the building beyond repair. The Monterey Fire Department suspected arson. Eventually, the state tore the old building down. Today, there's no plaque or modern interpretive panel to mark what happened there. But the legacy that Pop Ernest and his family left is still there.

The California commercial abalone fishery peaked in 1957 with more than 5.4 million pounds landed in California; in Monterey, just 10,333 pounds were landed, and by 1959, there were zero landings of abalone in Monterey. At one time, Monterey was the epicenter of the California abalone fishery, but that had now shifted to Southern California. But the commercial fishery continued mostly in Southern California and the

Santa Barbara area. Between 1950 and 1970, close to 4.5 million pounds of abalone were taken by commercial divers just in Southern California.

When Jacques Cousteau introduced the Aqua-Lung in 1948, anyone could go out and get abalone. All you had to have was a tank, a wet suit and a little training, and you were ready to go. In the '50s and early '60s, sport diving for abalone was a favorite pastime for many Californians. And most of the abalone that these sport divers were taking was being prepared and cooked Pop Ernest style, whether they knew it or not. These sport divers were taking so much abalone that by 1970, it was almost impossible to find any in the intertidal zone.

Throughout the '70s, '80s and '90s, the abalone fishery, both commercial and sport, really began to decline. There are several reasons for this decline, and overfishing is just one of them. A small raft of sea otters, which were thought to be hunted to extinction in the nineteenth century, were discovered off the coast near Point Sur by a man named Howard Granville Sharpe in March 1938. At the time of Mr. Granville's discovery, Japanese divers had been working that area for many years and had already become quite familiar with these "lost" otters. Otters, which must eat at least one-third of their body weight every day, particularly like abalone and would very often try to take the abalone from the diver or go after the diver's abalone basket as it was being pulled to the surface. These Japanese divers called these otters "sea cats." With this new discovery, the sea otter became federally protected, and as its population grew, the abalone population decreased, at least in the Monterey Bay area.

There were also environmental issues that affected the abalone population, including at least two El Niño systems in the 1980s and 1990s. These weather systems create a warming of the ocean that causes the nutrient levels, which kelp depend on, to decrease, and many of the kelp beds withered. Since kelp is the main food source for the abalone, this had disastrous effects on the abalone population and the abalone industry, especially in Southern California. There was also a disease called "withering foot syndrome," which causes the abalone's body to shrink in size as the shell stays the same. Eventually, the abalone can no longer hold on to the rock and protect itself from predators. The disease comes from a bacterium that doesn't allow the abalone to digest its food, and as a consequence, it starves to death. Finally in 1997, the California Department of Fish & Game closed both commercial and sport diving for abalone south of the Golden Gate. Abalone can still be taken today in Northern California, but it's heavily regulated and controlled by Fish & Game. You can only free-dive for abalone (no tanks) and for your own personal use. The amount of abalone you can take varies every year, so it's advisable to check with the California Department of Fish & Game as to current regulations.

Of course, as the California abalone population decreased, the cost for abalone increased. It was still pretty cheap in the 1970s; you could get an abalone steak dinner on the Monterey Wharf for under ten dollars. Today, at that same restaurant, that abalone steak dinner is going to cost closer to seventy-five dollars! The demand for abalone has not changed since Pop Ernest first introduced it at his Alvarado Street restaurant in 1908. Today, most of the abalone you're going to eat is farm raised, an idea that Pop first had in 1925 that has come full circle.

There are three abalone farms in the Monterey Bay area raising abalone for restaurants and consumers all over the world. The Monterey Abalone Company and Pacific Abalone Farm are both based in Monterey. Monterey Abalone Company was founded in 1991 and raises red abalone in cages under the building at the end of the commercial wharf. Pacific Abalone Farm has its operations right in the Monterey Harbor. US Abalone is a land-based abalone farm and was founded by Earl Ebert and his son, David Ebert, in Davenport just north of Santa Cruz. Earl Ebert is considered by many to be the father of modern abalone farming (also known as mariculture). Earl was a biologist for the California Department of Fish & Game for many years at Granite Creek, just south of Carmel, where much of his work was on abalone. In an unpublished article, he and David wrote this about abalone farming:

> *The technology for farming abalone is fairly well-developed. Farming operations may be land-based, or in the sea. In the latter case the abalone are typically grown in cages. Land-based operations employ a variety of tanks for the various growth stages. There are five elements in a typical farming operation.*
>
> *1. Broodstock Management—Initial broodstock is acquired from natural populations, but returned following spawnings. Thereafter, broodstock is selected, based on growth, from progeny and off-spring from successive spawnings. Inbreeding is avoided. Spawning is chemically induced;*
>
> *2. Larval Cultivation—Ova are fertilized and distributed into hatching tanks. Following hatching the larvae are put in thru-flowing, filtered seawater rearing tanks. After approximately one week they have matured sufficiently for settlement;*

Pop with his beloved beer steins. This photo was taken right after Pop was granted the first beer license in Monterey when President Roosevelt signed the Cullen-Harrison Act in March 1933. *Pat Sands Collection.*

3. *Nursery—Nursery tanks also employ filtered, thru-flowing seawater. Also, they are "conditioned" with a thin layer of diatoms* [single-celled algae]. *A chemical is used to induce larval settlement. The abalone forage on the diatoms and remain in the nursery tanks for approximately six months whereby they average about ½ inch long;*

4. *Weaning—Floating plastic mesh baskets are usually employed that contain plastic habitats. The juveniles are provided with seaweeds. Giant*

kelp is their preferred diet. Juvenile remain in the baskets for about six months whereby they average about 1-inch long;

5. Grow-Out—Raceway tanks that may range from 8 to 12 feet or more long are used. Giant kelp continues to comprise their principal diet. The abalone remain in these tanks for 2 to 2.5 years whereby they are 3.5 to 4 inches long and ready for market. The abalone are marketed alive locally, statewide, as well other states and to the Orient—principally Japan.

Of course, none of this would exist today without the creativity of Pop Ernest Doelter and the recipe that he developed at his small restaurant in Monterey, the Café Ernest, in 1908. Without that recipe, the California abalone industry, at least for the Japanese, would have died in California in 1915. But he kept this industry alive and thriving for many years. In 2007, the Awa Museum in Tateyama, Chiba, Japan, mounted an exhibit called Abalone as Food and Beauty. I was honored to be the guest curator of that exhibit and was able to bring Pop's story to Japan and to the families of the divers who bravely left their homes and families more than one hundred years ago to sail across the Pacific to an unknown place called Monterey and dive for abalone, thus enabling them send money home. Pop created more than just the abalone steak. He created an industry. He created a culture. Today, in a small restaurant in Tateyama, Japan, they serve Pop Ernest–style abalone. Pop would have been proud. All hail the King!

Appendix A

A Japanese Abalone Diver in the Monterey Bay

By Roy Hattori, excerpted from an interview with Tim Thomas and Linda Yamane in November 1995.

EQUIPMENT

Most of our diving was done in late spring and summer. The diving suit I used was a regulation Navy suit, very difficult to work in because they were made of rubberized canvas and were so hard. Wherever it bent it tended to cut you—at the elbows, at the knees, a very uncomfortable suit as compared with the Japanese-made suits, which were like silk. Because the Japanese ones were so soft they didn't abrade so much and get chafed. Until we found the Japanese suits and found a way to order them, we used Navy suits, and those we had to start repairing, patching, even after the first trip. Each trip was five days long. Five days of wear on any suit will get folds on them because of that much water pressure, especially when you get ridges on them. We used regular patches and rubber cement, just like tire patches.

There were also the weights. I carried a 35-pound weight on the front and 30 pounds in the back. They were hooked on to the two nipples at the front of the plate. One hung over the shoulder plate to the back with a loop underneath where the rope went around and tied on the bottom. It would

Roy Hattori in his dive underwear at age eighteen. *City of Monterey, California History Room.*

be difficult to take it off by yourself, but it was made so that the dresser could dress you easily and the weights wouldn't flop around.

My shoes weighed 16 pounds apiece. There was a layer of steel, a layer of lead, and then a layer of wood. The top part of the shoe, which was made from old tires, was fastened onto the wood. My dad made my shoes. Every diver had his own shoes made. Point Lobos has some in the Whaler's Cabin.

We used to knock the abalones off the rocks with a pick. The handle was about 10 inches long, and the blade a piece of $\frac{1}{4}$-inch steel that had a bend in it. It was about 8 inches long so that we could get an approximate measure of the abalone with the blade; we didn't want to pick up a lot of small stuff. It had a wooden handle with a hole for a string to put around your wrist. There was a blacksmith who made the picks for us.

With that long pick we had leverage. And with that bend in there, you didn't have to go in and pry, you could just turn it and it would flip the abalone off. The leading edge was sharpened very thin. Everybody used the same type of pick; nobody used a straight pick. I'm very sure that the shape for the pick came from the Japanese divers, and they made the handles longer, I think, so that you'd get a little reach for getting abalones out of holes.

As we gathered the abalones, we put them in the baskets [which are made of seine twine and knotted like a net, with a wooden ring forming the opening]. The bottom opens, that's how we got the abalone out, not through the top. The bottom is made so you can open it up as much as you want, as long as the abalone doesn't fall through. With good-sized abalones you'd fit maybe 13 or 14 at the most. If they were smaller, you might fit 20 to 22. If you were in a good spot, you would open up the bottom of the basket and re-tie the bottom, then cram the abalone in. If you opened up the bottom, you could hold maybe 50 percent more. And that way the people around you wouldn't see how many baskets you were putting up.

Everybody dove in about the same area, so if there were three or four boats together and you hit a real good spot and remained on that spot for any length of time the other divers and tenders were always watching to see who was pulling up the most baskets and how big the baskets were. They always kept an eye out for that. If they were close enough, they'd see if your basket was real full or not and that's how they kept track of you. It was a competitive business and everybody was trying to get as much as they could.

If you were in a place where you have to run around to find the abalone and had too many in the basket, you'd get tired. So we'd tend to close down the basket so we wouldn't have too many abalone in it at one time. It made it much easier on the arms and legs for running under water.

When the basket was filled, you gave the signal to the boat. Our signal was 3 jerks. Most of the people used three jerks, then whoever was tending would throw out two or three fathoms of line to give you a little leeway, and tie an empty basket on the life line. He would jerk once and the diver would pull it down. Then, when he got to the basket he would know where to tie on the full one. Everybody used the same knot—they call it a "fisherman's knot." It's very quick to use, and you can untie it real easily. But it'll also take weight without slipping, which is very important when you've got a basket full of abalone.

The Japanese helmet was not that heavy. I never bothered to weigh a breastplate and helmet, but it was about half the weight of the American type. The regulation Navy hats were very heavy, but then they had all kinds of gear on them, too. The Japanese hats were all stripped down. The only thing actually projecting from the helmet was the release valve. With the exhaust valve you could adjust the flow of air going out by either tightening or loosening the valve. The helmet has a small loop on the back of the helmet and there's a small loop on the very back of the breastplate, too. You're supposed to put a pin in there so that the helmet will never come off accidentally under water. I myself never used the pin. My helmet had the thing taken out and they just put it on with what they call a bayonet mount. Like the lens on a camera, you don't unscrew them, just one quarter turn and it comes off.

In the old days the air hose was a regular black rubber hose, and it was made for pressure, but it was heavy. It sank in the water, so the tenders had to be very careful not to give you too much leeway with the hose, otherwise it dragged on the bottom. It was very difficult to maneuver. Then they came out with a new type of floating hose. It was real nice—the line went straight up, unless there was a current, but generally the line went straight up to the surface and so you didn't have too much air hose hanging around you. The Japanese went to the trouble of taking heavy canvas and covering every hose. They didn't wrap the canvas around, they took strips of canvas and whip stitched it all the way down. They did that all by hand. They went to a lot of trouble to keep the diver as safe as possible. These hoses came in 50-foot lengths, and they covered the whole hose with canvas to keep it from abrading. The canvas also tended to protect the rubber from the sun. Your life depended on the hose. On the west coast we never had a single incident of a Japanese diver dying from any accident caused by diving.

You got into the diving suit and the shoulder plate fit over the shoulders to make everything watertight. The helmet was bolted to it with wing nuts.

On all the Japanese boats, the diver had no control of his air supply. There was no valve on the belt or on the helmet itself; all the air was governed by one valve that was set in the morning. In the morning, you put the helmet on and the tender opened the valve and kept opening until the diver said, "Stop." The diver could tell by the sound of the hiss in the helmet how much air he was getting.

Everyone had problems with their ears when they went down and came up. When I first started diving, my ears killed me. I hit the bottom and I could hardly move. I was eighteen and had just graduated from high school, and I didn't have a man with diving experience telling me what to do. All they did was put the suit on me and then they tossed me overboard. So I asked some of the old divers and they taught me how I could put my nose up against something in my helmet and blow to pop the ears and release the pressure. When coming up, blowing your ears doesn't do any good because you're going against pressure that's releasing. But when you're going up, the pressure is not as bad, because it's releasing.

There was a piece of canvas on the inside like the lip of an apron and it tended to catch any water that might seep through the breast plate or anywhere else. Especially when you hit the exhaust valve with your head, sometimes if the pressure was low in your helmet, the water would come shooting in because the outside pressure is much higher than what you have inside your helmet. You always got water in through the helmet but I learned to keep pulling that piece of canvas up with my teeth so the water wouldn't drop down and get into my clothing. If your clothes got wet, you got cold. And when you had to dive through all the daylight hours you had to stay warm.

The Japanese divers went on a ladder that dropped from the bow down. The ladder pulled up with a block and tackle. When the Japanese divers wanted to move, they just layed on the ladder and pulled the ladder up so it was out of the water. Then the boat would go forward to change positions. I think this made it much easier for the tender to manage both the life line and the air line, which he had to do when the diver was going down or when he was on the bottom. It was easier for him to just stand up there and take care of the divers when they came up or went down with the ladder facing that way.

BOATS AND CREW

There was a tender boat and the mother ship. The reason they used the mother ship was to carry the "live" boxes, which carried anywhere from 5 to 7 dozen abalone in each box. And they had eighteen boxes altogether on the deck of these boats. That allowed them to stay out two or three extra days.

Most crews carried three men on top, but some carried four. One man was on the scull, one man tended the lifeline and one helped to pull the abalone baskets on board and measured and stored the abalone into the hold of the diving tender. Generally, it was three men on top and the diver. Those four men would live on the boat for 5 to 7 days, so there was always a big water tank on top of the pilot cabin. These boats were originally built as half-ringers and were made for mackerel fishing, so they weren't that fast. They all carried 40 horsepower marine engines and the cylinders were great big old things. The *Tanami* was our boat—my father bought the boat and then we fixed it for diving. Ray Siino's father built the boat for us.

We used the boom and winch and everybody had their winch set up with the front end of the flywheel on the main motor. On the main motor, the diving tender was bolted; onto the flywheel was bolted the motor for the air compressor. You had to start the main engine in order to get air compression, and they used boiler tanks for the air reserve. The maximum you could get into those things was about 40 pounds. So you were diving with a maximum of 40 pounds of air in a 10-gallon tank and going down to depths of 70 or 80 feet. It's hard to figure how they could get that kind of air down to you in a pressure, but it worked because when you used the air, the pressure gradually built from the tank to the diver through that hose. I've been in 80–90 feet of water and still had enough, except the only thing that happened that was the suit was pressing so much that your ribs actually got compressed.

We rarely went down more than 60 feet, because you can't spend time on the bottom at 60 feet. Abalone diving is something that you have to spend time on the bottom in order to get the abalone. And so you didn't want to stay in a place where you had to come up and decompress all the time. The way they decompressed in the old days, if you worked 50–60 feet of water for half an hour or so, they had to take you out, bring you to about 30 feet, and let you work out the pressure in 30 feet for a period of time. That was standard procedure for all Japanese divers. The men on top always watched the time and the depth that you were at in order to keep you healthy. They could tell how deep you were by the lifeline. They knew exactly how much line they had and exactly how many feet of hose and could tell, as long as there wasn't a real strong current running.

The man on the scull used a big sweep, like a big oar to keep the boat in place with the diver, without using the motor. The diver's bubbles were constant, so there was always a steady stream to let the sculler know where the diver was. The Japanese were very careful. A lot of the Caucasian divers died when the propellers cut their air hoses. It was very easy to do, especially when it became windy. But with a sculling oar they kept the boat in position without jeopardizing the diver's safety. The only thing they couldn't do with this type of sweep was move in reverse, but they always kept the nose into the wind anyway.

The Diver

At 30–40 feet, the diver could work almost all day without coming up to decompress. We tried to work where we could find the most abalone, and stay down the longest. I've had spells where I've been on the bottom three hours straight without coming up. And then there were other places where I was up every half hour saying, "Well, there's nothing here." And we'd have to move to another place.

We had to run on the bottom to find the abalone, and it's not easy. In the very beginning, you tend to use a lot of energy working against the water. But as you get more and more used to diving and get a little more skillful, you learn to use the currents and surge to give you the necessary impetus to travel a little bit faster and easier. And you tend to carry more air. In the beginning, you tend to let the air out of your suit more quickly so that you'll have more firmness on the bottom, so that you won't float around. But as you get more and more used to it, you use that air more. You keep the air in your suit and kind of float around, just giving little kicks, unless you were running on a sandy bottom.

You had to keep your body temperature up under water, so we wore two or three pair of knitted underwear. Most of the men did their own knitting; they took old sweaters apart and used the wool to knit the underwear. But my mother knitted most of mine.

The Abalone

Abalone move around all the time; they're forever looking for better feed. There was one place right below Granite Creek on Highway 1, where there was an abalone farm for awhile. That place has a bottom that is very rocky and they were not small rocks, but big, good-sized rocks with holes all over. In that one particular spot, I would go down and pick up 35 to 40 dozen in one day, every time I was there. The current there was very good, I think, so that they had a lot of good feed. If you took an abalone off of one spot, the next time you went back there was another one there, or very close to it. And so it showed that the abalone's always moving, looking for better food. And they can move pretty fast. I've seen abalone traveling on sand, which I really didn't believe at first, but they do travel on sand in certain spots—only when the current or the surge is not strong, though. They can't do it when the surge is strong because the sandy bottom always ripples, and if they overturned, they'd have nothing to fasten on to in order to right themselves, and they would die.

The abalone is actually just a big marine snail with a shell on its back, only it's a flat shell instead of conical. They just kind of glide over the rocks and if they're moving, like over the bottom where there's a lot of marine growth, you can just lift them up without even using a pick. And if they're feeding, the shell is up and the lip part is out searching for kelp, and you can just pull them off the rocks without using a pick. But if they sense you or if you touch them, they'll clamp down or they'll increase the suction of their foot and if they're on a flat surface it's very difficult to get them off. When you get used to them, you learn to use the pick really quick to take them off. They must feel vibrations, too, because if you hit the rock they'll clamp down.

THE LIVE BOXES

When the abalone were brought up, they were put into the "live" boxes, which held anywhere from five to seven dozen abalone each. The boxes were made with big spaces in between each plank, and when they were lowered into the water the water circulated through them to keep the abalone alive. For the first two or three days, we put the abalone catch into these live boxes and put them in the water, on a line tied to the stern of the mother ship. After that, we lined all the abalone on deck and covered them with mats, throwing water on the mats to keep them moist so they wouldn't dry out. We could do that for two days. After that, you had to come in, because if you didn't your abalone were going to start dying.

BRINGING THE ABALONE IN

After coming into port, we emptied all the boxes and threw all the abalone up against the cabin so we'd have a little room on the deck for the winch to put down the boxes. From the market on the wharf, they would winch down this box. We put in so many dozen and each time they'd take it up and dump it onto a truck, a hand truck, and then the hand truck would go inside where the processors would process it.

The fishermen were paid by the dozen—we got a dollar and-a-half a dozen, regardless of the size. The biggest abalone I remember getting was about eleven and three-eighths inches, and that's a big abalone. The processor paid all the people who worked processing the abalone and pounding them. And then he sold them by the pound to the wholesaler. The ladies pounded all day long. It's a wonder that they could do it, but they did.

We took those shells by the thousands and trucked them out to Seaside, just about where the Monterey Beach Hotel is and just dumped them on the dunes there. Everybody dumped their shells out there—thousands and thousands of them.

A Different World

When I was a kid I used to swim out in the bay and I would look down and see these black dark spots where the kelp were and think, "Gee, you know, you don't know what's down there." It's really kind of scary when you're swimming on the surface and you can't see under water. But when I became a diver, I realized how different that world was. It's such a different world once you get your face under water. It's so beautiful. There are so many things to see that you could sit by a rock under water and spend a whole day and see something different every minute!

Abalone Recipes

Pop Ernest's Abalone Steak

Slice the foot off of the abalone to make the steak. Pound, lightly, but firmly, three or four times, with a wooden mallet or rolling pin. Do not over-pound or your steak will be too soft. Season with salt and pepper and abalone nectar (the juice that comes from the shell) run through an egg wash, finely crushed cracker crumbs and cook quickly in butter or olive oil no more the 45 seconds per side, serve.

The above is the author's take on Pop's famous recipe.

According to Peter Howorth, author of the *Abalone Book*, the following Pop Ernest recipe was on a sign attached to the old Pop Ernest restaurant building in the late 1960s:

1 pound sliced, tenderized abalone steaks
1 teaspoon freshly ground pepper
1 beaten egg
3 tablespoons dry sherry
½ cube of butter

Slices of the meat placed on a hard surface are pounded with a heavy wooden mallet or rolling pin to break the tissue. Without a properly spirited

APPENDIX B

pounding, the abalone is too tough to eat, but, if assaulted too savagely, it becomes mush. The slices are dipped in beaten egg thinned with dry sherry, then fried in butter in a heavy skillet, one minute to a side.

The following recipes come from the Point Lobos Canning Company label. Point Lobos worked with the head chef at the Hotel Del Monte in Monterey, who developed these recipes circa 1915, just in time for the Panama Pacific International Exhibition. You can still find canned abalone in most Asian markets today.

ABALONE SOUP
To the contents of this can add one pint of hot water or milk, season to taste with butter, salt and pepper.

ABALONE SALAD
To the meat of one can of abalone and a little celery and onion, mix with mayonnaise dressing, serve on crisp lettuce leaves.

ABALONE CROQUETTES (DEL MONTE STYLE)
To the meat of one can, season with red pepper, salt, and add a little finely chopped onion and parsley, mix with cream sauce, let cool, shape and dip in egg then fry in deep fat.

ABALONE CHOWDER (DEL MONTE STYLE)
Cut in small dice two ounces of pickled pork, two medium sized potatoes and chop up fine a good sized onion. Fry the pork for five minutes to a light brown color, then add the onions and cook for five minutes. Put two quarts of water into a vessel and the contents of two cans of abalone add a little thyme and one bay leaf and bring to a boil. Put it on one side of range and let simmer for half an hour. Season to taste. Just before serving work in one ounce butter and add one cup good rich cream.

ABALONE FRITTERS (DEL MONTE STYLE)
The contents of the can and ½ the juice, one cup of flour, two eggs, salt, pepper a pinch of sugar and one teaspoon baking powder. First mix the abalone, flour and seasoning thoroughly together. Then put in the juice and eggs, the baking powder to be worked in last. Fry in a pan well-buttered.

ABALONE RECIPES

ABALONE COCKTAIL
Empty the contents of can a can of abalone, season with cocktail sauce to taste.

The following two recipes come from *Five Hundred Ways to Prepare California Sea Foods*. This booklet was published in 1933 by the State of California State Fish Exchange to promote the eating of fresh California seafood.

CREAMED ABALONE

Serves 2.

One and one-half cup-full of flaked abalone that has been cooked. Make a white sauce by heating two tablespoons of butter in a saucepan. Stir until bubbling, add two tablespoons of flour which has been seasoned with one quarter teaspoonful of salt and one-eighth teaspoonful of pepper, and stir until blended with the butter. Heat one cupful milk and pour gradually over butter and flour. Stir until smooth and creamy. Mix this sauce with one raw egg yolk. Hard boil one egg. Stir sliced white of egg into mixture, pour on toast and sprinkle with grated egg yolk.

FRIED ABALONE

Abalone may be procured from dealer already prepared for cooking. Wipe dry and season with salt and pepper. Dip abalone in a beaten egg and then fine bread crumbs. Heat olive oil over a moderate fire and when quite hot, place abalone in a pan and fry only until browned slightly on both sides. Care must be taken that the pan does not become too hot. (This is "Pop" Ernest Style)

APPENDIX B

SMOKED KELP, MARINATED RED ABALONE WITH LOCAL SEA VEGETABLES

Recipe from Chef John Cox of the Sierra Mar at the Post Ranch, Big Sur

Servings 4 (appetizer size)

For the Abalone:
4 small Monterey red abalone
2 blades of fresh kelp
1 tablespoon rice wine vinegar powder
1 tablespoon Monterey sea salt
1 tablespoon Togarashi spice mix

1. Remove the abalone from shell using a spoon.
2. Remove the frills and digestive tract from abalone.
3. Scrub abalone with damp towel to remove some of the black coating.
4. Cold-smoke the kelp for 1 hour.
5. Season the kelp with rice vinegar powder, sea salt and Togarashi.
6. Lay the abalone on top of one of the seasoned kelp leaves.
7. Top with the other leaf and either cryovac or press overnight.
8. Refrigerate overnight.
9. Slice paper-thin and layer on parchment paper.

For the Sea Vegetables:
5 cups ice water
8 ounces of assorted freshly foraged seaweeds (bull kelp, sea grapes, Turkish towel, Ogo, Chainbladder, sea lettuce, etc.).
2 cups rice wine vinegar
1 teaspoon chopped ginger
1/2 teaspoon chopped Thai chile
1 cup sugar
3 cloves garlic

1. Bring a large pot of water to a boil (no salt). Blanch the sea vegetables for 5 seconds then transfer immediately to ice water. Remove and dry.
2. Bring remaining ingredients to simmer. Steep for ten minutes. Strain. Cool.
3. Put the blanched sea vegetables in pickling brine overnight. Hold for up to one week.

For the Vinaigrette:
1 lime, juiced
1 yuzu, zested
1 teaspoon white tahini paste
1 jalapeño finely chopped
1 teaspoon microplaned ginger
2 tablespoons white soy sauce
2 tablespoons rice wine vinegar
2 tablespoons rice oil

1. Combine all ingredients in mortar and pestle and mix until emulsified.

ASSEMBLING

1. Clean the abalone shells. Arrange the paper-thin slices of abalone in a loose floret on top of shell.
2. Dress the pickled seaweeds with vinaigrette.
3. Top abalone with the seaweeds.

ABALONE, NORI, WHITE ALBA MUSHROOMS, PUFFED RICE

Recipe from Chef Justin Cogley of L'Auberge Carmel

Ingredients:
abalone
abalone mushrooms
nori sauce
rice cracker
nori powder
sunflower sprout

PREPARATIONS
FUMET BLANC
45 grams butter
100 grams shallot

80 grams celery root
100 grams leek
150 grams vermouth
1 liter fumet
600 grams cream
60 grams mushroom
200 grams crème fraîche

Sweat the first four ingredients in the butter until tender. Once tender, deglaze with the vermouth and cook out the alcohol. Add the fumet and bring to a boil. Reduce to a simmer and let cook for 45 minutes. Add the cream and mushrooms and bring back to a boil. Strain and temper in the crème fraîche. Season with cayenne, lime juice and salt. Strain and reserve.

ABALONE
Clean and pound. Sous-vide for 25 minutes at 65 degrees Celsius. Shock in ice water.

NORI SAUCE
Lightly toast several sheets of nori and place in a blender with enough water to turn the mixture. Blend to smooth and pass through a chinois.

NORI POWDER
Grind the nori in a spice grinder until powdered.

ABALONE MUSHROOMS
Sauté on pick up with butter, finish with chives.

RICE CHIP
400 grams sushi rice
squid ink
25 grams 5-spice powder
kombu pieces (any left over)

Overcook rice until soft and the moisture is gone. Blend in a vita prep and spread on silpat. Swirl in squid ink to make marble effect. Dry above the oven until crispy. Fry in 375-degree oil until puffy. Drain on towels to remove excess oil. Season with fine salt and serve.

ABALONE RECIPES

Pop's Abalone Stew

This recipe is from The Abalone Lover's Cookbook, *second edition, by Jeri Siegel and Michael Hill.*

One of Pop's signature dishes was his abalone stew. Unfortunately, we don't have his recipe, but it was probably similar to the recipe below, with two important variations. "Pop" would have used canned abalone, and his stew didn't use tomato sauce but most likely milk or cream. And I doubt he used cayenne pepper.

⅓ cup butter, unsalted
1 large clove of garlic, minced
⅓ cup bell pepper, chopped
1 cup onion, chopped
1 bay leaf
2 cups water
8 ounces tomato sauce
3 potatoes, peeled and cut into ½-inch cubes
½ teaspoon salt
⅓ teaspoon cayenne pepper
1 pound raw abalone, tenderized and cut into small cubes

In a saucepan, melt the butter and sauté the garlic, bell pepper and onion until the onion is transparent. Add the bay leaf, water, tomato sauce, potatoes, salt and cayenne and then cover and simmer about 15 minutes. Add the abalone and simmer 4 to 5 minutes until tender. Serves 8.

Abalone, Meuniere Style, with a Seaweed Persillade

Recipe from David Kinch, Manresa Restaurant, Los Gatos, California

For the Persillade:
3 ounces extra virgin olive oil
1 small onion, peeled and diced fine
1 small clove garlic, chopped fine

1 cup seaweed "laitue de mer," soaked in cold water and rinsed clean
1 tablespoon capers, chopped fine
1 tablespoon champagne vinegar
lemon zest

For the Abalone:
4 small abalone, approximately 4–5 ounces each in shell weight
1 cup of dashi (Japanese seaweed stock)
1 cup flour
3 ounces sweet butter
1 tablespoon lemon juice
sea salt, to season

To Prepare the Persillade:
This can be done one day in advance. Place 1 ounce of olive oil in a pan and place it over a low heat. Add the onions and sauté, stirring occasionally. Make sure they don't color. Add the chopped garlic and continue to cook and stir until the onions are completely soft. Remove the mixture from the pan and allow it to cool in a bowl. Chop the seaweed fairly fine and stir into the cool onion mix along with the capers. Taste and see if it needs a pinch of salt. The salt might not be needed because of the natural salinity of the capers and seaweed. Finish seasoning with champagne vinegar, the last of the oil and the lemon zest. It should have the consistency of a loose paste.

To Prepare the Abalone:
The day before: Using a large tablespoon, shuck the abalone from its shell by going behind the abalone and forcing out the "foot" from the bottom of the shell. Slice off the innards that are at one end of the abalone so it is clean. You might have to pinch the end to expose the last bit of entrails attached. Put the abalone on a plate, cover with plastic wrap and place in the refrigerator overnight. This step will relax the abalone and prevent it from splitting when it is pounded.

The day of serving: Lay out a tea towel on a sturdy table or butcher's block. Remove the abalone from the fridge and make crosscut incisions about 1/4-inch apart and 1/4-inch deep on the bottom of the foot of the abalone. Place the abalone foot side down on the edge of the tea towel and fold the other edge of the towel over the abalone to completely cover them. Pound each abalone two to three times gently but firmly with a meat pounder. Do not use a tenderizer or the meat cuber side of a pounder. Use only a flat, even surface. You should slightly flatten the abalone without disfiguring or splitting it. Return the abalone to its plate and cover with plastic wrap.

Heat the dashi until just below a simmer. Have it at the ready. When ready to serve, toss the abalone in flour and shake off all the excess flour. Do not season with salt in advance as they tend to have a high natural salinity. Heat all the butter in a good sauté pan over medium-high heat. When the butter stops sizzling and begins to foam, add the abalone to the pan, foot side up. Gently shake the pan constantly and allow the butter to slowly turn to a hazelnut brown with a nutty aroma. After about 2 minutes, turn the abalone and finish another minute on the foot side. The abalone and the butter should both be golden brown. Add the lemon juice and shake the pan to coat with the juices.

Place a spoonful of the *persillade* on top of the finished abalone and spread the mixture to cover the entire surface of the abalone. Place the abalone in a shallow bowl and pour just enough dashi broth to come up the sides of the abalone without submerging it. Serve immediately. *Serves 4.*

MONTEREY ABALONE ROCKEFELLER

From Burt Cutino, co-owner and chef of the Sardine Factory, Monterey, California.

Preparation:
6 ounces cultured baby abalone (2-ounce portions, 1 inch cut)
3 cultured abalone shells (3 inches each)
3 tablespoons spinach mixture (see recipe)
3 tablespoons mushroom duxelles mixture (see recipe)
3 tablespoons mousseline sauce (see recipe)
1 tablespoon fresh chives, chopped
garnish three shells with three cups of rock salt and three sprigs of seaweed

Procedure: Clean shells thoroughly. In each shell, put 1 tablespoon of spinach mixture, 2 ounces of abalone and then 1 tablespoon of mushroom duxelles mixture on top. Add mousseline sauce and cook under broiler 5 minutes in hot oven.

For the Spinach Mixture:
1 cup spinach, cleaned
1 teaspoon garlic, chopped
1 teaspoon shallots, chopped
½ teaspoon lemon juice
1 ounce white wine
1 pinch salt
1 pinch pepper
1 teaspoon butter

Procedure: Steam cleaned spinach in steamer. Rinse in cold water. Drain well. In a pot, sauté garlic and shallots until soft; add all other ingredients except butter and mix well. Cook about 3 minutes. Add butter and mix well. Let cool well before using.

For the Mousseline Sauce:
4 each egg yolks
2 tablespoons white wine
1¾ cups clarified butter, warmed
½ teaspoon lemon juice
½ teaspoon Worcestershire sauce
½ teaspoon Tabasco sauce
½ teaspoon salt
½ teaspoon pepper
3 ounces whipping cream, whipped stiff

Procedure: Start Hollandaise sauce in clean metal bowl with egg yolks and white wine. Begin whisking quickly over a boiling pot of water. Continue whisking until eggs begin to triple in volume and a glaze begins to form on the egg. After 15 to 20 minutes of continued beating, the mixture will become viscous and start to thicken. At this point, start adding warmed clarified butter to egg mixture off of flame. Add gradually and continue to whisk vigorously until all of the butter is incorporated. Add lemon juice, Worcestershire sauce, Tabasco sauce, salt and pepper to Hollandaise. Fold in whipped cream until homogenous.

For the Mushroom Duxelles Mixture:
1 tablespoon garlic, finely diced
2 tablespoons shallots, finely diced

¼ pound domestic mushrooms, thinly sliced
4 ounces Madeira wine
8 ounces heavy cream
¼ cup demi stock, reduced
2 tablespoons roasted red peppers, diced
1 teaspoon parsley, chopped fine
¼ cup green onions, finely diced
1 teaspoon Worcestershire sauce
½ teaspoon caramel coloring
¼ cup butter roux, cooked until tan color
1 pinch salt
1 pinch white pepper

Procedure: In a pot, sauté garlic and shallots until soft. Add mushrooms and stir well. Add Madeira wine and cook down for 5 minutes. Add cream and reduced demi stock; add red peppers, parsley, onions, Worcestershire sauce and caramel color. Let cook for 10 minutes. Then add butter roux and let cook slowly for 10 minutes. Finish with salt and white pepper and pour into a large pan to let cool.

Recommended Wines: Talbott Sleepy Hollow Chardonnay 2010, Monterey County, California, and Bernardus Sauvignon Blanc 2011, Carmel Valley, California.

Appendix C

Abalone and Japanese Cooking

Recollection and Memoir of the Tradition

By Takeshi Suzuki, Gyotakuso-Suzuki-ya in Chikura, Minami-Boso City

I have been running a small traditional style inn named Gyotakuso-Suzuki-ya in my native town Chikura. The inn was founded by my great grandfather in 1899 and, there, is as old as 115 years. Perhaps, it is the oldest in Chikura and its neighboring area. Our guests have the opportunities for staying and eating traditional seafoods including Abalone from the area. The inn is located in central Chikura, quite close to the Pacific seacoast, and is surrounded by many open fields of cultivated flowers, which bring in spring colors in winter time ahead of season.

In my childhood, abalones and langoustines were regularly captured here in Chikura, but they were rather high priced and were not our daily foods. An exception was in May when the seasonal ban on capturing them was lifted, a woman diver (or "ama") of our neighborhood brought some of her captures to my family and we enjoyed eating them. I remember that abalone was mostly served as "sashimi" (sliced raw meat) or sautéed with butter. When it was served as "sashimi," its shell was used as a plate as shown in the picture. Retrospectively thinking, such a way of serving abalone brought in a pleasant atmosphere. On a special occasion such as when my relations visited my family, abalone was cooked as "saka-mushi," or sake-steamed (see recipe below), and served.

The chef of Gyotakuso-Suzuki-ya was in Tateyama City and is quite familiar with the traditions in this area. According to him, abalone is cooked in "saka-mushi" with radish to make its meat tender and light soy sauce and "mirin" are used only in a small amount to add a subtle flavor and enhance the abalone's taste.

Some of the old traditions still exist in the Chikura area: for example, on the occasion of spring and autumn festivals, a "houchou-skiki," or a ceremonial way of slicing fish, abalone, etc. with a sword-like kitchen knife without touching them with hands, will be performed at Takabe Shrine in Chikura. I have been working as a guide of the ceremony to explain details of the process to those watching it.

A Typical Recipe for "Saka-Mushi" (or Sake-Steamed) Abalone at Gyotakuso-Suzuki-ya

1. Wash fresh abalone (with the shell attached) thoroughly in running water.
2. Pour one volume of water and two volumes of sake into a saucepan.
3. Place the washed abalone (after removing the shell) and several pieces of sliced radish. Cook them for 3 ½ hours on low heat.
4. Add "light soy sauce" and "mirin" to fix the taste.
5. Cook for a further 30 minutes on low heat to complete.

Additional Remarks

Besides the saka-mushi of abalone described above, there are other traditional cookings of abalone in Japan such as "nigai" (literally, cooked abalone) in Yamanashi Prefecture, which is an inland prefecture located west of Tokyo. Because of its location, salt and seafoods had to be transported mainly from its southern neighbor, Shizuoka Prefecture. There is a legendary saying that as abalone dipped in soy sauce for preservation was transported for several tens of kilometers on horseback, by the time it reached Yamanashi, people found that abalone had been nicely processed in soy sauce and became quite tasty. Since then, "nigai" in Yamanashi acquired its reputation.

Also, since ancient times, half-dried abalone was peeled and repeatedly pressed into a thin strip of more than a meter in length, which was called "noshi" and regarded to bring a good fortune and long life. It was recorded in a book from the 10th century that a "noshi" so prepared in Boso (southern Chiba Prefecture including Chikura) was transported and donated to a central Shinto shrine Nara. Even today, "noshi" is frequently attached to a package of a gift or to an envelope containing money to be given to a couple getting married, though it is a decorative paper-made imitation.

Index

INDEX

About the Author

Tim Thomas, fourth-generation native of the Monterey area, is a fisheries historian who has researched the fisheries of Monterey Bay for twenty-five years. He has researched, written and lectured extensively on Monterey's fishing communities and for sixteen years was the historian/curator at the Monterey Maritime Museum. Tim is the co-author (with Dennis Copeland) of *Monterey's Waterfront*, published in 2006, and the author of *The Japanese on the Monterey Peninsula*. He is also on the board of directors of the Monterey Japanese American Citizens League and has traveled and lectured extensively on the Monterey Japanese community both here and in Japan. Tim is also a popular local tour guide and owner/guide of Monterey Waterfront & Cannery Row Tours.